I Believe

Bruce R. McConkie

A Retrospective of
Twelve Firesides and Devotionals
Brigham Young University
1973–1985

Order from
Speeches
218 UPB
Brigham Young University
Provo, UT 84602
http://speeches.byu.edu

Editor's Note: Since the 1950s the editorial methods for BYU speeches have gradually matured. Most of the speeches in this custom book appear as originally published.

CONTENTS

Agency or Inspiration—Which?

Bruce R. McConkie

I've been many places with my wife when, as we have met members of the Church, stake presidencies, high councils, and the like, they've said to me: "We're surely glad to meet you, Brother McConkie, and we're most pleased to have Sister Smith with us." I've assured her that that was all right with me, as long as they didn't call me Brother Smith. And now that's happened.*

I've sought the Lord diligently, as is my custom, to be guided and directed this morning in what ought to be said—sought him both for myself and for you, so that I might speak and you might hear by the power of the Holy Spirit. Two subjects have occurred to me. I thought that on the one hand I might talk about "Agency or Inspiration—Which?" Or, on the other hand, I might talk about how to choose a wife. It occurred to me I might consult the student body, but then I said to myself, "No, it doesn't make a particle of difference which subject it is; I'm going to say exactly the same things anyway."

---

*In the introduction, Elder McConkie was inadvertently referred to as "Elder Smith."

This devotional address was given at Brigham Young University on 27 February 1973.

My wife and I were having a serious discussion recently, in which we were counting our many blessings. We named a host of things that have come to us, because of the Church, because of our family, because of the glorious restoration of eternal truth that has taken place in this day; and then she climaxed the discussion by asking this question: "What's the greatest blessing that has ever come into your life?"

Without a moment's hesitation I said, "The greatest blessing that has ever come to me was on the thirteenth day of October in 1937, at 11:20 a.m., when I was privileged to kneel in the Salt Lake Temple at the Lord's altar and receive you as an eternal companion."

She said, "Well, you passed that test."

I believe that the most important single thing that any Latter-day Saint ever does in this world is to marry the right person, in the right place, by the right authority; and that then—when they have been so sealed by the power and authority which Elijah the prophet restored—the most important remaining thing that any Latter-day Saint can ever do is so to live that the terms and conditions of the covenant thus made will be binding and efficacious now and forever. And so I'd like, if properly guided, to make some suggestions that apply in all fields of choice—in all fields, at least all major fields, of activity—but which apply particularly to the matter of eternal marriage, singling that out as the one thing paramount above all others.

When we dwelt in the presence of God our Heavenly Father, we were endowed with agency. This gave us the opportunity, the privilege, to choose what we would do—to make a free, untrammeled choice. When Father Adam was placed in the Garden of Eden, he was given this same power, and we now possess it. We're expected to use the gifts and talents and abilities, the sense and judgment and agency with which we are endowed.

But on the other hand, we're commanded to seek the Lord, to desire his Spirit, to get the spirit of revelation and inspiration in our lives. We come unto the Church and a legal administrator places his hands upon our head and says, "Receive the Holy Ghost."

This gives us the gift of the Holy Ghost, which is the right to the constant companionship of that member of the Godhead, based on faithfulness.

And so we're faced with two propositions. One is that we ought to be guided by the spirit of inspiration, the spirit of revelation. The other is that we're here under a direction to use our agency, to determine what we ought to do on our own; and we need to strike a fine balance between these two, if we're going to pursue a course that will give us joy and satisfaction and peace in this life and lead to eternal reward in our Father's kingdom.

When we were with our Father in the preexistent sphere, he observed and studied us; he knew how we would respond to his laws when we were in his presence, when we had the knowledge that he was our Father and that the teachings presented to us came from him. We walked by sight. Now he's finding out how we'll respond when we walk by faith, when we're outside his presence and we have to rely on other things than the personal counsel that we once received from him.

Well, I'd like, if I may, to present three case studies, out of which, perhaps, we can draw some very realistic and sound conclusions as to what ought to be in our lives. I'll take these illustrations out of the revelations that the Lord has given us.

"YOU HAVE NOT UNDERSTOOD"

Case study number one: There was a man named Oliver Cowdery. In the early days, he operated as an amanuensis to the Prophet. He was the scribe. He wrote down the words that the Prophet dictated while the Spirit rested upon him in the translation processes (the Book of Mormon was then being translated). Brother Cowdery was relatively spiritually immature at that time, and he sought and desired to do something beyond his then present spiritual capacity. He himself wanted to translate. And so he importuned the Prophet, the Prophet took the matter up with the Lord, and they got a revelation. The Lord said, "Oliver Cowdery, verily, verily, I say unto you, that assuredly as the Lord liveth, who is your God and your

Redeemer, even so surely shall you receive a knowledge of whatsoever things you shall ask in faith, with an honest heart, believing that you shall receive." And then one thing he might receive is defined as "a knowledge concerning the engravings of old records, which are ancient, which contain those parts of my scripture of which as been spoken by the manifestation of my Spirit" (D&C 8:1).

Having thus dealt with the specific problem, then the Lord revealed a principle that applies to it and all other like situations: "Yea, behold, I will tell you in your mind and in your heart, by the Holy Ghost, which shall come upon you and which shall dwell in your heart. Now, behold, this is the spirit of revelation" (D&C 8:2–3).

Well now, Oliver did what a good many of us would have done. He had the instructions I have read, and he assumed that they meant what they seemed on the surface to say, which was that if in faith he asked God he'd have power to translate. But in his condition of relative spiritual immaturity, he hadn't yet learned what was involved in asking of God, or how to generate the kind of faith or do the specific thing that has to be done in order to get an answer to a prayer. And so he asked. And as you know, he failed; he was totally unable to translate. This caused some concern, I suppose, to him and the Prophet. The matter was referred back to the Lord, whose promise they had been attempting to conform to; and the answer came, the reason came, why he couldn't translate: "You have not understood; you have supposed that I would give it unto you, when you took no thought save it was to ask me" (D&C 9:7).

Now, seemingly, that's all he'd been instructed to do, to ask in faith; but implicit in asking in faith is the precedent requirement that we do everything in our power to accomplish the goal that we seek. We use the agency with which we have been endowed. We use every faculty and capacity and ability that we possess to bring about the eventuality that may be involved. Now this is translating the Book of Mormon, it's choosing a wife, it's choosing employment, it's doing any one of ten thousand important things that arise in our lives.

The Lord continued:

I say unto you, that you must study it out in your mind; then you must ask
me if it be right, and if it is right I will cause that your bosom shall burn
within you; therefore, you shall feel that it is right.

But if it be not right you shall have no such feelings, but you shall have
a stupor of thought that shall cause you to forget the thing which is wrong;
therefore, you cannot write that which is sacred save it be given you from
me. [D&C 9:8–9]

How do you choose a wife? I've heard a lot of young people
from Brigham Young University and elsewhere say, "I've got to get a
feeling of inspiration. I've got to get some revelation. I've got to fast
and pray and get the Lord to manifest to me whom I should marry."
Well, maybe it will be a little shock to you, but never in my life did
I ever ask the Lord whom I ought to marry. It never occurred to me
to ask him. I went out and found the girl I wanted; she suited me; I
evaluated and weighed the proposition, and it just seemed a hundred
percent to me as though this ought to be. Now, if I'd done things
perfectly, I'd have done some counseling with the Lord, which I
didn't do; but all I did was pray to the Lord and ask for some guidance and direction in connection with the decision that I'd reached.
A more perfect thing to have done would have been to counsel with
him relative to the decision and get a spiritual confirmation that the
conclusion, which I by my agency and faculties had arrived at, was the
right one.

"WHY ARE YOU ASKING ME?"

Now, case study number two: There was a man whose name is
not so much as preserved to us in the ancient record. He's known
as the brother of Jared. From other sources we know his name was
Moriancumer. He was the spiritual leader, initially, of the Jaredite
people. As they started their progress from the Tower of Babel to
their American promised land, he was the one that got in communion
with the Lord to get the direction, the spiritual guidance, that they,
as a people, needed.

And some very interesting things occurred. They got to the waters that they were going to cross, and the Lord said to him, "Build some barges." But interestingly, the Lord didn't tell him how to build the barges. The brother of Jared had done it on a previous occasion; he didn't need instruction; there wasn't any revelation that was necessary to guide him. So he built the barges.

But this time they were going to be used under some peculiar and difficult circumstances, and the brother of Jared needed something more than was now present in them: he needed some air. And this was a problem that was beyond him. So he took that matter up with the Lord, and because it was totally beyond his capacity to solve, the Lord solved it for him and said, "Do thus and so and you'll have air."

But then the brother of Jared—having confidence because he was talking to the Lord, because he was communing and getting answers—asked another question: he asked for a solution to a problem that he should have figured out by himself and not taken up with the Lord. He said, "What will we do for light in the vessels?"

And the Lord talked to him about it a little and then he said this: "What will ye that I should do that ye may have light in your vessels?" (Eth. 2:23). In effect, "What are you asking me for? This is something you should have solved." And he talked a little more, and he repeated in essence the question: "What will ye that I should prepare for you that ye may have light when ye are swallowed up in the depths of the sea?" (Eth. 2:25). In other words, "Moriancumer, this is your problem. Why are you troubling me? I've given you your agency; you are endowed with capacity and ability. Get out and solve the problem."

Well, the brother of Jared got the message. He went up into a mount called Shelem, and the record says he "did molten out of a rock sixteen small stones; and they were white and clear, even as transparent glass" (Eth. 3:1).

I hold here a little piece of amorphous quartz that's clear as transparent glass. I picked this up in a wilderness area outside of a little community called Crystalina, in a nation called Brazil, in South America. The Brethren thought I was off touring missions, but actually I was doing a little rock hunting. And in that connection, I hope you got the message that the brother of Jared was a rock hound also.

Well, the brother of Jared took sixteen little crystals of some sort (he could hold all of them in his hands); he took them up on the mount. The record says, "He did carry them in his hands upon the top of the mount" (Eth. 3:1), and then he said in effect to the Lord, "Now this is what I hope you will do." You really don't tell the Lord what to do, but you get some inspiration and you use your judgment, and then you talk the matter over with him. And so Moriancumer said to the Lord: "Touch these stones, O Lord, with thy finger, and prepare them that they may shine forth in darkness; and they shall shine forth unto us in the vessels which we have prepared, that we may have light while we shall cross the sea" (Eth. 3:4).

And the Lord did what the brother of Jared asked, and this is the occasion when he then saw the finger of the Lord; and, while he was in tune, he received revelation that exceeded anything that any prophet had ever gained up to that moment. The Lord revealed more to him about his nature and personality than ever theretofore had come forth, and it all came about because he'd done everything that he could do and because he counseled with the Lord.

There's a fine balance between agency and inspiration. We're expected to do everything in our power that we can, and then to seek an answer from the Lord, a confirming seal that we've reached the right conclusion; and sometimes, happily, in addition, we get added truths and knowledge that we hadn't even supposed.

"THEY SHALL COUNSEL BETWEEN THEMSELVES AND ME"

Now case study number 3: In the early history of the Church, the Lord commanded the Saints to assemble in a certain place in Missouri. The decree went forth: "Assemble." Specifically, the decree went forth, "Let the Presiding Bishop come here and do such and such." Now notice what happened. The Lord is talking:

As I spake concerning my servant Edward Partridge, this land is the land of his residence, and those whom he has appointed for his counselors; and also the land of the residence of him whom I have appointed to keep my storehouse;

Wherefore, let them bring their families to this land, [and here's the point] *as they shall counsel between themselves and me.* [D&C 58:24–25]

You see, the Lord said "assemble" to Zion. The details and the arrangements, however, the *how* and the *when* and the *circumstances* are to be determined by the agency of those who are called to assemble, but they are to counsel with the Lord. Now, when you counsel with the Lord, you talk something over. I bring my children in and we counsel on a problem. I don't tell them what ought to be; I say, "What do you think? What's your evaluation? What do you want to do in this situation? What's the best thing to do?" And they tell me what they think, and if I happen to have any wisdom or judgment on the matter, I express my views. Well now, the Lord has all wisdom, all knowledge, and all power; he knows how to govern and control and direct us in a perfect manner. He lets us determine what we should do, but he expects us to counsel with him.

Now, after the Lord had said this to the Presiding Bishopric of the Church, he gave the principle that governed in that situation, and it governs in all situations. And this is one of our glorious revealed truths. He said:

For behold, it is not meet that I should command in all things; for he that is compelled in all things, the same is a slothful and not a wise servant; wherefore he receiveth no reward.

Verily I say, men should be anxiously engaged in a good cause, and do many things of their own free will, and bring to pass much righteousness;

For the power is in them, wherein they are agents unto themselves. And inasmuch as men do good they shall in nowise lose their reward.

But he that doeth not anything until he is commanded, and receiveth a commandment with doubtful heart, and keepeth it with slothfulness, the same is damned. [D&C 58:26–29]

You know, they said to the Prophet Joseph Smith, "How do you govern so great and diverse a people as the Latter-day Saints?"

He said, "I teach them correct principles, and they govern themselves."

Now, that's the order of heaven. That's how the Almighty operates. That's how the Church is supposed to operate. We're supposed to learn correct principles and then govern ourselves. We make our own choices, and then we present the matter to the Lord and get his approving, ratifying seal.

"COUNSEL WITH THE LORD IN ALL THY DOINGS"

Now, those are the three case studies; let us come to the revealed conclusion. There was a man named Alma, a mighty and a great prophet. He had a son named Helaman, who was a holy and righteous man, following the pattern that his father had set. And to Helaman, Alma said this: "O, remember, my son, and learn wisdom in thy youth; yea, learn in thy youth to keep the commandments of God. Yea, and cry unto God for all thy support" (Al. 37:35–36). Do you think that if you're counseled to pray to the Lord for support, both temporal and spiritual, that that's all you have to do? The Lord's prayer says, "Give us this day our daily bread" (Matt. 6:11). Do you go out and sit down in the desert or on the mountain and pray with all the fervor you can possess, "Give us this day our daily bread," or do you go out and plant crops and raise herds and do everything that you can in your situation to accomplish the end result?

Well, continuing: "Yea, let all thy doings be unto the Lord, and whithersoever thou goest let it be in the Lord; yea, let thy thoughts be directed unto the Lord; yea, let the affections of thy heart be placed upon the Lord forever" (Al. 37:36). Now note: "Counsel with the Lord in all thy doings, and he will direct thee for good" (Al. 37:37).

What was Oliver Cowdery's problem? "You took no thought save it was to ask. . . .You must study it out in your mind" (D&C 9:7–8).

Well, do you want a wife? Do you want anything that's right and proper? You go to work and you use the agency and power and ability that God has given you. You use every faculty, you get all the judgment that you can centered on the problem, you make up your own mind, and then, to be sure that you don't err, you counsel with the Lord. You talk it over. You say, "This is what I think; what do you think?" And if you get the calm, sweet surety that comes only from the Holy Spirit, you know you've reached the right conclusion; but if there's anxiety and uncertainty in your heart, then you'd better start over, because the Lord's hand is not in it, and you're not getting the ratifying seal that, as a member of the Church who has the gift of the Holy Ghost, you are entitled to receive.

"Yea, when thou liest down at night lie down unto the Lord, that he may watch over you in your sleep; and when thou risest in the morning let thy heart be full of thanks unto God; and if ye do these things, ye shall be lifted up at the last day" (Al. 37:37). If you learn how to use the agency that God has given you, and if you try to make your own decisions, and if you reach conclusions that are sound and right, and you counsel with the Lord and get his ratifying seal of approval upon the conclusions you've reached, then you've received revelation, for one thing; and for another thing, you're going to have the great reward of eternal life, be lifted up at the last day. Now, we're not all equal by any means; some have one talent and capacity and some another. But if we use the talents we have, somehow we'll come out all right.

On the recent Monday when we were celebrating Washington's birthday, I was down at my mother's sawing a log in the backyard. She came out to give me some direction and see how I was doing it, and she wasn't very pleased. She thought I ought to do it differently. She went back into the house and in a few minutes my younger brother arrived. She said to him, "I think you'd better go out in the backyard and give Bruce some help and see that he does this thing right." And then she said to him, "Bruce isn't very bright." Well, so I'm not. So I start where I am, and I go forward from there. I start using such talent as I have, and I begin to apply principles of eternal truth to my life. And I consult and counsel with the Lord in the process. And no matter where I am, the gospel takes me forward and onward and upward, and blessings flow to me that will ennoble and sanctify and improve me in this life and eventually give me glory and honor and dignity in the life to come.

WE HAVE THE SPIRIT OF REVELATION

Now, I think we've said enough; the principles are before us. Let me just do one thing more. Let me do, in effect, what my friend Alma would do. After he'd preached a sermon, he said, "And this is not all. Do ye not suppose that I know of these things myself?" (Al. 5:45). That is, he'd given them the case studies, he'd quoted the revelations, he'd told them what was involved, and then he bore personal testimony. This is what we ought to do in the Church. We ought to learn how to teach by the power of the Spirit, so that when we get through talking about the gospel subjects we'll know whether what we've said is right, and we'll be in a position to bear testimony, not alone of the truth and the divinity of the work, but also that the doctrine we proclaim and the everlasting truths which we expound are right, that they are the mind and voice and will of the Lord. Now, the glorious, wondrous thing about this work and about these doctrines is that they are true. There isn't anything in this world, no truth that we can conceive of, to compare with the truth that the work we're engaged in is true, that the Lord's hand is here. It's a literal fact that we have the gift and power of the Holy Ghost. We have the spirit of revelation, the spirit of testimony, the spirit of prophecy. These things must be, or else we're not the church and kingdom of God; we're not the Lord's people.

Now, the fact is that we do have them; revelation works. Don't shy away from getting revelation. Joseph Smith said, "God hath not revealed anything to Joseph, but what He will make known unto the Twelve, and even the least Saint may know all things as fast as he is able to bear them" (*Teachings of the Prophet Joseph Smith*, p. 149). We're entitled to the spirit of revelation. But what I'm attempting to teach this morning is that there's a how and a procedure, and there are conditions precedent, and it is our obligation to go to work on our problems and then counsel with the Lord and get the ratifying seal of the Holy Spirit on the conclusions that we've reached; and that ratifying seal is the spirit of revelation.

God grant us wisdom in these things. God grant us the courage and the ability to stand on our own feet and use our agency and the abilities and capacities we possess; then let's be sufficiently humble and amenable to the Spirit to bow our will to his will, to get his ratifying, confirming seal of approval, to get in our lives, in that way, the spirit of revelation. And if we so do, there's no question about the result: it's peace in this life; it's glory and honor and dignity in the life to come. Which may God grant for all of us. In the name of Jesus Christ. Amen.

Succession in the Presidency

Bruce R. McConkie

I am pleased and honored to have this privilege of meeting and worshiping with you in your devotional services as you commence the new year. I devoutly and sincerely desire the guidance and enlightenment that comes from the Holy Spirit—first for me, so that I may say what ought to be said and what the Lord would have said on this occasion; and secondly for you, so that your hearts may be open and receptive and so that you may feel the truth and verity of the expressions that will be made.

President Dallin Oaks has indicated, appropriately, the passing of President Harold B. Lee, one of the great spiritual giants of our dispensation. I would like, if I may properly be guided, to talk to you about succession in the presidency and to let you have a feeling and an understanding of what is involved when the Lord calls a prophet to other spheres of activity.

Let us begin with the sure and certain conviction in our souls that this is the Lord's work. This is the Lord's church, and he is running it. There isn't any question at all about that. As President

This devotional address was given at Brigham Young University on 8 January 1974.

Oaks indicated, the Lord calls his prophets and the Lord releases
his prophets. No prophet can be called by any other power, and no
prophet can be released by any other power.

And so, for reasons that are not wholly and completely known
to us, although we do have some vision and understanding of what is
involved, on Wednesday, December 26, 1973, the Lord reached forth
his hand and touched his servant, President Harold B. Lee. President
Lee had been in good health; he had been vigorous and active up to
that point in his life. But on that day the Lord said to him: "Come
hither. I have other work for you to do in another sphere. I have
greater labors and a greater work for you here than you've been
doing in mortality."

CALLINGS TO THE OTHER SIDE OF THE VEIL

Difficult as it is for us to envision fully why President Lee was
taken, we have no difficulty in accepting it and in understanding that
he is going forward in the Lord's work in another sphere. I would
like to read a statement by President Wilford Woodruff relative to
the passing of the noble and good and faithful from this life into the
labors that await them in the realms ahead. President Woodruff says:

> *The same Priesthood exists on the other side of the vail* [sic]. *Every
> man who is faithful in his quorum here will join his quorum there. When a
> man dies and his body is laid in the tomb, he does not lose his position. The
> Prophet Joseph Smith held the keys of this dispensation on this side of the
> vail, and he will hold them throughout the countless ages of eternity. He
> went into the spirit world to unlock the prison doors and to preach the Gospel
> to the millions of spirits who are in darkness, and every Apostle, every
> Seventy, every Elder, etc., who has died in the faith as soon as he passes to
> the other side of the vail, enters into the work of the ministry, and there is
> a thousand times more to preach there than there is here.*

I think President Woodruff's next comment has particular
application to President Lee's passing:

I have felt of late as if our brethren on the other side of the vail had held a council, and that they had said to this one, and that one, "Cease thy work on earth, come hence, we need help," and they have called this man and that man. It has appeared so to me in seeing the many men who have been called from our midst lately. [Journal of Discourses, 22:333–34]

When President Lee passed he was attended by President Marion G. Romney, his second counselor, and President Spencer W. Kimball, the President of the Council of the Twelve. President N. Eldon Tanner was in Arizona at the time. Brother Romney, as the representative of and counselor to President Lee, was in complete and total charge at the hospital. He gave President Lee a blessing. He felt the spirit of peace and satisfaction, the calm assurance that whatever eventuated would be right. He did not promise President Lee that he would be healed. The President had become ill very rapidly, just in a matter of hours or moments. Shortly after this blessing, he passed away. At the moment he passed, Brother Romney, in harmony with the system and the established tradition and custom of the Church, stepped aside, and President Spencer W. Kimball was then in complete charge and had total direction. President Kimball was at that moment the senior apostle of God on earth. And as the last heartbeat of President Lee ceased, the mantle of leadership passed to President Kimball, whose next heartbeat was that of the living oracle and presiding authority of God on earth. From that moment the Church continued under the direction of President Kimball.

THE ESTABLISHED PROCEDURE FOR SUCCESSION

It was not required, nor was it requisite or needed, that the Lord give any revelation, that any special direction be given. The law was already ordained and established. God does not look down each morning and say, "The sun shall rise." He has already established the law, he has set the sun in the firmament, and the sun operates in harmony with established law in its rising. And so it was with the transfer of leadership from President Lee to President Kimball.

When the President of the Church passes on, the First
Presidency is disorganized, and the mantle of leadership—the reins
of presidency—go to the senior man left and to the Council of the
Twelve as a body; in effect the Council of the Twelve then becomes
the First Presidency of the Church and so continues unless and until
a formal reorganization takes place. These words I read to you from
President Joseph F. Smith:

> *There is always a head in the Church, and if the presidency of the
> Church are removed by death or another cause, then the next head of the
> Church is the Twelve Apostles, until a presidency is again organized of
> three presiding high priests who have the right to hold the office of First
> Presidency over the Church; and, according to the doctrine laid down by
> President Wilford Woodruff, who saw the necessity for it, and that of
> President Lorenzo Snow, if the President should die, his counselors are then
> released from that presidency, and it is the duty of the Twelve Apostles to
> proceed at once, in the manner that has been pointed out, to see that the
> First Presidency is reorganized, so that there may be no deficiency in the
> working and order of the priesthood in the Church of God.* [*Conference
> Report*, April 1913, pp. 4–5]

Harmonious with that policy, that counsel, and that instruction—
which has been followed in previous instances—the Council of the
Twelve met in the upper room of the Salt Lake Temple on Sunday,
December 30, at 3:00 p.m. for the purpose of reorganizing the First
Presidency of the Church. Normally in that upper room there are
three chairs occupied by the First Presidency and twelve chairs in a
semicircle in front of them occupied by the members of the Council
of the Twelve. On this occasion, however, there were fourteen chairs
in the semicircle, because there were fourteen Brethren present who
had been sustained and ordained and set apart as members of the
Council of the Twelve.

We took our places in those chairs, and President Kimball
presided in the meeting, which lasted for about 3½ hours. In the
course of this meeting President Kimball explained the business to

be transacted, the things that might be done if the Brethren felt so guided and led. He explained that when the Prophet Joseph Smith was martyred, 3½ years went by before President Young was formally chosen and installed as President of the Church. He noted that almost that period went by between President Young and President John Taylor and between President Taylor and President Wilford Woodruff but that in each succeeding instance the time had varied from four to eleven days, and we were meeting on the fourth day after the passing of President Lee.

He expressed himself as to what should be done, and he said that the proposition to be first considered was whether the First Presidency should then be reorganized or whether the Church should continue to function with the Council of the Twelve as its presiding officers. He then invited each member of the Twelve, commencing with Elder Ezra Taft Benson and continuing around the circle to me, to arise in turn and express himself frankly and fully and freely as to what ought to be done. I'll tell you what in thought-content and substance was said by all of the Brethren on that occasion, but if I may, let me preface my statement by reading an account of what happened in the meeting of the Council of the Twelve on the first occasion when they considered the problem of reorganizing the First Presidency of the Church. There have, of course, been eleven such meetings in this dispensation. These words I now read were spoken by Elder Orson Hyde of the Council of the Twelve as he told of the first meeting:

In the month of February, 1848, the Twelve Apostles met at Hyde Park, Pottawattamie County, Iowa, where a small Branch of the Church was established. . . . We were in prayer and council, communing together; and what took place on that occasion? The voice of God came from on high, and spake to the Council. Every latent feeling was aroused, and every heart melted. What did it say unto us? "Let my servant Brigham step forth and receive the full power of the presiding Priesthood in my Church and kingdom." This was the voice of the Almighty unto us at Council Bluffs, before I removed to what was called Kanesville. It has been said by some that Brigham was appointed by the people, and not by the voice of God.

I do not know that this testimony has often, if ever, been given to the masses of the people before; but I am one that was present, and there are others here that were also present on that occasion, and did hear and feel the voice from heaven, and we were filled with the power of God. This is my testimony; these are my declarations unto the Saints—unto the members of the kingdom of God in the last days, and to all people.

. . . Men, women, and children came running together where we were, and asked us what was the matter. They said that their houses shook, and the ground trembled, and they did not know but that there was an earthquake. We told them that there was nothing the matter—not to be alarmed; the Lord was only whispering to us a little, and that he was probably not very far off. We felt no shaking of the earth or of the house, but were filled with the exceeding power and goodness of God. We knew and realized that we had the testimony of God within us. On the 6th day of April following, at our Annual Conference [I might say that on the coming sixth day of April at our annual conference, we'll do precisely what they did here], *held in the Log Tabernacle at Kanesville, the propriety of choosing a man to preside over the Church was investigated. In a very few minutes it was agreed to, and Brigham Young was chosen to fill that place without a dissenting voice, the people not knowing that there had been any revelation touching the matter. They ignorantly seconded the voice of the Lord from on high in his appointment.* (Voice from the stand: "That is, *Vox Dei, vox populi.*") *Yes, the voice of God was the voice of the people. Brigham went right ahead, silently, to do the work of the Lord, and to feed his sheep, and take care of them like a faithful shepherd, leaving all vain aspirants to quarrel and contend about lineal descent, right, power, and authority.* [*Journal of Discourses,* 8:233–34]

That is what transpired the first time that the Council of the Twelve met to reorganize the First Presidency of the Church. And in essence, thought-content, and certainly in spirit, precisely the same thing occurred on the thirtieth day of December last. Each member of the Council in turn, specifically and pointedly, expressed himself to the effect that now was the time to reorganize the First Presidency of the Church, that there should not be further delay, that the effective and proper operation of this great organization that we have from the Lord needed this administrative arrangement. Each one in turn expressed himself that President Spencer W. Kimball was the man whom the Lord wanted to preside over the Church; there was no question whatever about that. There was total and complete unity and harmony. The prayer that was in the heart of every person present was "Lord, show unto thy servants whom thou hast chosen to be President of the Church." We did not want to do anything other than what the Lord wanted done.

President Young is quoted as having said, following the death of the Prophet, "I don't care who presides in the Church. All I want to know is what the Lord thinks about it." The Lord made manifest his will in that day, and that's all we wanted to know for our day. And when we met for this most recent reorganization, the Lord made manifest his will to us. It was as though the voice of God had said to each one of us individually and to all of us collectively: "Let my servant Spencer step forth and receive the full power of the presiding priesthood in my Church and kingdom."

THE ORDINATION OF PRESIDENT KIMBALL

And so after there had been full expression and consideration, Elder Ezra Taft Benson, the next one in seniority to President Kimball, made the formal motion that the First Presidency of the Church be reorganized; that President Spencer W. Kimball be sustained, ordained, and set apart as the President of the Church; as the prophet, seer, and revelator to the Church; and as the Trustee-in-Trust. This motion was adopted unanimously.

At this point President Kimball made a speech of acceptance—a very sweet, humble, appropriate expression. In the course of our meeting he had explained, as he did at President Lee's funeral, that no man had prayed more sincerely and devoutly, with more feeling and desire, for the life, vigor, health, and continued spiritual and physical prosperity of President Lee than he had done. But President Kimball was willing to accept the will of the Lord and the mantle of leadership that had fallen upon him.

At this point, he chose his first counselor, President N. Eldon Tanner, who responded appropriately and sweetly; he then chose President Marion G. Romney to be the second, who similarly responded. Following these appointments, Brother Benson was sustained as the President of the Council of the Twelve. And then all those present placed their hands upon the head of President Kimball, and he was ordained and set apart, with President Benson being mouth, to serve as President of the Church and as the prophet, seer, and revelator for this time and this season.

Now President Lee has passed away. He was a great spiritual giant, a prince in Israel, someone to whom we looked with unbounded admiration. Few men have lived in our day who have had more direct contact with the Lord, who have felt the spirit of inspiration and who have been able to convey the mind and will of the Lord to his people as well as President Lee has done. We had supposed, not knowing the providences of the Lord, that President Lee would be with us for a long time. But there are two things we should note in his call to go elsewhere. One is that the Lord has another work for him to do, and it is a greater and more extensive work than what he was presently assigned to do. The Lord, in his infinite wisdom and goodness, knows what ought to be done with his servants. The other thing to note is that when the Lord calls a new prophet he does it because he has a work and a labor and a mission for the new man to perform.

I can suppose that when the Prophet Joseph Smith was taken from this life the Saints felt themselves in the depths of despair. To think that a leader of such spiritual magnitude had been taken from them! Our revelation says, "Joseph Smith, the Prophet and Seer of the Lord, has done more, save Jesus only, for the salvation of men in this world, than any other man that ever lived in it" (D&C 135:3). We do not have language or capacity or ability to extol the greatness and the glory of the ministry and mission of the Prophet Joseph Smith. And yet when he was taken the Lord had Brigham Young. Brigham Young stepped forth and wore the mantle of leadership. With all respect and admiration and every accolade of praise resting upon the Prophet Joseph, still Brigham Young came forward and did things that then had to be done in a better way than the Prophet Joseph himself could have done them.

Now, no one can say too emphatically or too strongly or praise too highly the leadership of President Lee, but this is a forward-looking Church. We do not look backward. We do not do other than go forward and onward. Our destiny is to proclaim the everlasting gospel into every ear. This Church will roll on until the knowledge of God covers the earth as the waters cover the sea. And so we look to the future. We now look to a new prophet who will wear the mantle of leadership and who will, with dignity and honor and inspiration and with the guidance of heaven, do things that are appointed for his time and his season that no one else could have done. The Lord's hand is in the work, and Spencer Kimball is the prophet of God, the mouthpiece of the Almighty for the time and the season that are appointed ahead. God grant that it may be extensive and long and that we may continue to get the inspiration and guidance that come through his newly appointed servant.

KEYS OF PRESIDENCY

Now, this is the pattern; this is the system. Succession in the presidency happens in an orderly and systematized way, because the Lord has conferred upon the members of the Council of the Twelve all of the keys and powers and authorities that have ever been held in any dispensation or any age of the past. Every key is given to each apostle who is set apart a member of the Council of the Twelve. But because keys are the right of presidency, they lie dormant, as it were, in each man unless and until he becomes the senior apostle and is thus in a position of presidency to direct the labors and the work of all others. Therefore succession occurs, as it were, automatically.

Let me turn again to Wilford Woodruff, who spoke so eloquently and accurately on this, and let you feel, as I read, the spirit of that great prophet and the message he gave:

We had had our endowments; we had had all the blessings sealed upon our heads that were ever given to the apostles or prophets on the face of the earth. On that occasion the Prophet Joseph rose up and said to us: "Brethren, I have desired to live to see this temple built. I shall never live to see it, but you will. I have sealed upon your heads all the keys of the kingdom of God. I have sealed upon you every key, power, principle that the God of heaven has revealed to me. Now, no matter where I may go or what I may do, the kingdom rests upon you."

. . . "But," he said, after having done this, "ye apostles of the Lamb of God, my brethren, upon your shoulders this kingdom rests; now you have got to round up your shoulders and bear off the kingdom." And he also made this very strange remark, "If you do not do it you will be damned.". . .

When the Lord gave the keys of the kingdom of God, the keys of the Melchizedek Priesthood, of the apostleship, and sealed them upon the head of Joseph Smith, he sealed them upon his head to stay here upon the earth until the coming of the Son of Man. Well might Brigham Young say, "The keys of the kingdom of God are here." They were with him to the day of his death. They then rested upon the head of another man—President John Taylor. He held those keys to the hour of his death. They then fell by turn, or in the providence of God, upon Wilford Woodruff.

I say to the Latter-day Saints, the keys of the kingdom of God are here, and they are going to stay here, too, until the coming of the Son of Man. Let all Israel understand that. They may not rest upon my head but a short time, but they will then rest on the head of another apostle, and another after him, and so continue until the coming of the Lord Jesus Christ in the clouds of heaven to "reward every man according to the deeds done in the body.". . .

. . . I say to all Israel at this day, I say to the whole world, that the God of Israel, who organized this Church and kingdom, never ordained any President or Presidency to lead it astray. Hear it, ye Israel, no man who has ever breathed the breath of life can hold these keys of the kingdom of God and lead the people astray. [Discourses of Wilford Woodruff, ed. G. Homer Durham (Salt Lake City: Bookcraft, 1946), pp. 72–74]

THE DESTINY OF THE CHURCH

And that conclusion of President Woodruff's is implicit in the
eternal decree that the gospel is to roll forth, that the Church is to
remain, that this time there will never be apostasy, but that we are
preparing a people for the second coming of the Son of Man. Let
me read you the words that the Lord said to Joshua when Moses was
taken:

*There shall not any man be able to stand before thee all the days of thy
life: as I was with Moses, so I will be with thee: I will not fail thee, nor
forsake thee.*

Be strong and of a good courage. [Joshua 1:5–6]

Now, in effect, the Lord has said that to Spencer W. Kimball.
And as the Lord was with President Harold B. Lee, so he will be with
his newly called servant—that humble and sweet and gracious and
wonderful man, President Spencer W. Kimball. The problem is not
one of what happens where the Church is concerned. The destiny of
the Church is guaranteed and assured. The only problem that ever
can arise is with individuals—whether individuals will walk in the
light and do the things that they must do to be in harmony with the
Church and to reap and inherit its blessings.

I have attempted very simply and informally to recite to you what
took place and to recount and set forth the principle that is involved.
What I have said is true and accurate. It is proper and it is appropriate that these things should be known to us. Now I think every one
of us needs to know in his heart of the truth and divinity of the work
and have a testimony and assurance that what has gone forward is
right and is the mind and will of the Lord. All of the Twelve have
that. That is the beginning. It spreads forth from them to all Israel.
I bear testimony because the Holy Spirit of God has revealed it to
my soul that President Spencer W. Kimball is the Lord's anointed
for the time and season ahead. And because God is no respecter of
persons, everyone in the Church who will get on his knees and ask
the Lord for guidance and direction will receive identically that same

knowledge, that same assurance, and that same understanding. And those who have this assurance will have a foundation for continued righteousness and devotion and for that course of conduct which brings peace in this life and eternal life in the world to come, which may God grant for all of us in the name of the Lord Jesus Christ. Amen.

The Ten Commandments
of a Peculiar People

Bruce R. McConkie

Thank you, President Oaks. I am honored and delighted to have this opportunity to meet and worship with the student body and faculty of Brigham Young University on this occasion. I have pondered and prayed much to learn what the Lord wants me to say to the youth of Zion, to the young and rising generation of the Church. My prayer has been and is "O God, manifest unto thy servant what thou wouldst have said to those who are a choice and a peculiar treasure unto thee above all the peoples of the earth." In response, there has come into my heart the desire to consider our unique and peculiar status as members of the only true and living church upon the face of the whole earth. If I may now be guided by the Spirit, I shall take up the doctrine that we are a peculiar people; show wherein that peculiarity lies; tell how it may be obtained and perfected; and draw some conclusions as to what is expected of us because of our unique status.

This devotional address was given at Brigham Young University on 28 January 1975.

WE ARE A PECULIAR PEOPLE

There is an old saying, "All the world is queer save me and thee, and sometimes I think even thee is a little queer." This is used jocularly of those who set themselves apart from mankind and who profess to be or seemingly are different from other people. We do not place ourselves in this category. We are not freaks, but normal, wholesome people who enjoy life. We work and play, engage in sports, mingle with other people, go to parties, and enjoy festive occasions. But we are, nonetheless, peculiar in the eyes of worldly people. We are a breed set apart. We are different from the world because we do not ape the practices and follow the fashions of worldly and carnal people. We glory in the things which set us apart by ourselves, and we hope and pray that we may maintain and increase the differences. Of the true saints, with whom we are numbered, Peter said: "But ye are a chosen generation, a royal priesthood, an holy nation, a peculiar people." Having so announced, he told what is expected of them: "That ye should shew forth the praises of him who hath called you out of darkness into his marvellous light" (1 Peter 2:9).

Query: How shall we show forth the praises of him who called us out of darkness into his marvelous light? This is equivalent to asking, "How do we worship the Lord?"

Answer: It is more than in song or sermon; perfect worship is emulation. Perfect praise is to do the things he would have us do. It is to keep the commandments of God.

To true saints, and we are they, Paul wrote:

For the grace of God that bringeth salvation hath appeared to all men,
Teaching us that, denying ungodliness and worldly lusts, we should live soberly, righteously, and godly, in this present world;
Looking for that blessed hope [the hope of eternal life], *and the glorious appearing of the great God and our Saviour Jesus Christ;*
Who gave himself for us, that he might redeem us from all iniquity, and purify unto himself a peculiar people, zealous of good works. [Titus 2:11–14; emphasis added]

Query: How does the Lord purify unto himself a peculiar people?

Answer: He does it when that people forsake ungodliness and worldly lusts, when they live soberly, righteously, and godly, in this present world. He does it when that people take counsel from him and keep his commandments.

To his chosen Israel, of whom we are a part, the Lord said: "If ye will obey my voice indeed, and keep my covenant, then ye shall be a peculiar treasure unto me above all people: for all the earth is mine: And ye shall be unto me a kingdom of priests, and an holy nation" (Exodus 19:5–6). Note the terms of the Lord's offer: "Obey my voice; keep my covenant." This covenant is the fulness of his everlasting gospel. It is the new and everlasting covenant in which we promise to forsake the world and in which he promises us an inheritance with him in his Father's kingdom. All those who keep the covenant, who live by gospel standards, receive this promise: "For thou art an holy people unto the Lord thy God, and the Lord hath chosen thee to be a peculiar people unto himself, above all the nations that are upon the earth" (Deuteronomy 14:2). And I say to you, "You are that people—'an holy people,' a chosen and favored people, a people set apart, 'a peculiar people.'"

THE FAMILY OF THE LORD

Now, with those principles before us, may I speak of the special family relationship enjoyed by those who so live that they become a peculiar people. Of them it is written: "Ye are the sons of the living God" (Hosea 1:10). That is, those who gain the high status of a peculiar people are adopted into the family of the Lord Jehovah. They become his sons and his daughters and have him as their father. Our best recitation of the doctrine here involved is found in these words of King Benjamin:

And now, because of the covenant which ye have made [in the waters of baptism] *ye shall be called the children of Christ, his sons, and his daughters; for behold, this day he hath spiritually begotten you; for ye say that your hearts are changed through faith on his name; therefore, ye are born of him and have become his sons and his daughters.* [Mosiah 5:7]

This is a special family relationship reserved for the faithful. It is over, above, and in addition to the fact that all men are the spirit children of the Eternal Father.

King Benjamin continues:

And under this head ye are made free, and there is no other head whereby ye can be made free. There is no other name given whereby salvation cometh; therefore, I would that ye should take upon you the name of Christ, all you that have entered into the covenant with God that ye should be obedient unto the end of your lives.

And it shall come to pass that whosever doeth this shall be found at the right hand of God, for he shall know the name by which he is called; for he shall be called by the name of Christ. [Mosiah 5:8–9]

This is a glorious and wondrous doctrine. We are the sons and daughters of the living God, the children of the great Jehovah, the adopted offspring of the Lord Jesus Christ. We bear the name of Christ. We are members of his family. He is our father. Now, how do we gain such a personal relationship with him who has bought us with his blood? He says:

But to as many as received me, gave I power to become my sons; and even so will I give unto as many as will receive me, power to become my sons.

And verily, verily, I say unto you, he that receiveth my gospel receiveth me; and he that receiveth not my gospel receiveth not me.

And this is my gospel—repentance and baptism by water, and then cometh the baptism of fire and the Holy Ghost, even the Comforter, which showeth all things, and teacheth the peaceable things of the kingdom. [D&C 39:4–6]

When we partake of the sacrament, we renew the covenants made in the waters of baptism. We agree again to take upon ourselves the name of the Son and to keep his commandments so we shall always have his Spirit to be with us.

Baptism and the sacrament are the ordinances which open the door so that as a people, peculiar and set apart from the world, we have power to become sons and daughters of God. Obeying and conforming, denying ungodliness and worldly lusts, living soberly and righteously and godly in this present world—such a way of life is the course whereby the power is exercised and the desired eventuality obtained.

In my father's family we had a saying, "Remember who you are and act accordingly." I adopted this same motto for my family. My wife tells me that her father did precisely the same thing. Our family motto meant to us, "First, you are a McConkie; you have been taught the truth; you know what is expected of you at all times; you are to live by the standards of the family and avoid anything that would stain the family name. Second, you are a Christian; Jehovah is your shepherd; the Lord Jesus is your father; you are to live by gospel standards and not do anything which would bring disrepute upon him whose name you bear; you are to keep his commandments."

Now, in the light of the principle that we are a peculiar people who have become the sons and daughters of him who is our Lord, may I suggest some specific things that will help us overcome the world and make the doctrines here involved live in us. I shall do this by presenting what we may term the ten commandments of a peculiar people. First the commandments and then a brief commentary about them.

BE VIRTUOUS

The first commandment: *Thou shalt be morally clean and conform to every standard of virtue and chastity.*

The commentary: People who live after the manner of the world are immoral and unclean—so much so that we sometimes wonder whether there are any moral standards left among men. People speak of a new morality, which is, in fact, immorality under a new name. We are confronted on every hand—on radio, on television, in the movies, and in the so-called literature that is available—with a recitation of standards that are contrary to gospel principles. They are inherent in the course that the world pursues.

But the true Saints still adhere to the divine decree, "Thou shalt not commit adultery" (Exodus 20:14). We still believe "that whosoever looketh on a woman to lust after her hath committed adultery with her already in his heart" (Matthew 5:28). Our proclamation still is "thou shalt love thy wife with all thy heart, and shalt cleave unto her and none else. And he that looketh upon a woman to lust after her shall deny the faith, and shall not have the Spirit" (D&C 42:22–23). Immorality is the crying evil of our day. It ranks next to murder in the category of personal sins. We must shun it, avoid it, flee from it. It destroys men spiritually in this life and sends them to an endless hell in the life to come. The word of the Lord given to the world through us still is "For I, the Lord God, delight in the chastity of women. And whoredoms are an abomination before me; thus saith the Lord of Hosts" (Jacob 2:28).

BRIDLE YOUR PASSIONS

The second commandment: *Thou shalt bridle thy passions and abstain from all manner of lasciviousness.*

The commentary: We are here in mortality to be tried and tested; we are on probation. The great test is whether we overcome the lusts of the flesh, flee from that which is lewd, and live by gospel standards. We are to overcome the world. If we get involved in necking and petting, if we go to pornographic movies, if we read trashy and vulgar books or magazines, if we tell or enjoy vulgar stories, if we profane and are unclean in thought or word, we are living after the manner of the world. Then there is nothing peculiar about us. We are as the generality of mankind. We are outside the family circle. We lose our status as the sons and daughters of our Lord. Oh that it might be said of us as it was of them of old:

There was no contention in the land, because of the love of God which did dwell in the hearts of the people.

And there were no envyings, nor strifes, nor tumults, nor whoredoms,
nor lyings, nor murders, nor any manner of lasciviousness; and surely there
could not be a happier people among all the people who had been created by
the hand of God. [4 Nephi 15–16]

What an accolade that is! "Surely there could not be a happier people
among all the people who had been created by the hand of God."
True happiness is found only in righteous conduct. No one can live
after the manner of the world and be truly happy. "Wickedness never
was happiness" (Alma 41:10).

BE MODEST

The third commandment: *Thou shalt be modest in dress and*
appearance.

Commentary: It may come as a surprise to some people to learn
that modesty in dress and grooming is related to salvation. I left the
Missionary Executive Committee meeting this morning to come
here, and the last item approved was a document to go to mission
presidents, stake presidents, and bishops instructing each to counsel all returned missionaries to conform to the dress and grooming
standards that had prevailed in their missions.

The Bible has a great deal to say about covering our nakedness,
about costly and ornate apparel, about excessive use of jewelry, about
garish and worldly costumes, and, yes, about hair styles. Women are
told to avoid "plaiting" the hair and not to wear "broided hair." I suggest you figure out what those things mean in the context where they
were used by Peter and Paul. The Holy Book approves long hair for
women and short hair for men: "Doth not even nature itself teach
you," Paul says, "that, if a man have long hair, it is a shame unto
him?" (1 Corinthians 11:14). I noted in the Church section of the
Deseret News that within the month President Spencer W. Kimball,
speaking before a similar group, quoted that sentence from Paul with
the same application that we're making here.

Conformity to dress and grooming standards is one of the tests the
Lord imposes upon us to see if we will take counsel and to see if we

can stand up against the pressures of the world. There is, of course, an underlying reason for all the counsels and commands relayed from the Lord by the Brethren to the Saints. Immodesty, for instance, leads toward immorality. Long hair and grubby grooming open the door to rebellion against the established order and to associations which lead away from the Church. Surely those who are so adorned are not living soberly, righteously, and godly in this present world. But even if we are not sufficiently in tune to recognize the valid reasons behind the dress and grooming standards, we are still expected to abide by them. We might well hark back to the counsel given Adam to offer sacrifices. He, not knowing the underlying reasons, did so in order to conform to the counsel that the Lord gave. And in due course the angel from heaven explained what was involved (see Moses 5:5–8).

BE HONEST

The fourth commandment: *Thou shalt be honest and manifest integrity in all thy doings.*

The commentary: The devil whispers to men, "Lie a little; there is no harm in a little dishonesty; a little stealing won't matter; everybody cheats on an exam, and you have to in order to get by; don't search out the true owner of lost property; learn to get along in the world by living the way worldly people live." We are living in a day when evil is on the increase. Shoplifting, crime, and dishonest practices prevail in increasing measure throughout the world. In my judgment this will continue until the day of the coming of the Son of Man, when the wicked will be destroyed, the earth will be regenerated, and we will have a new way of life. I think also that in the midst of these worldly circumstances the Church itself, at least the faithful portion of it, is being perfected. We are living by higher standards, and we are preparing ourselves to be that people who will be ready for the Lord when he comes again. As to these matters, the Lord our God has never rescinded that which is written: "Thou shalt not steal" (Exodus 20:15). No amendment has ever been appended to the decree "Wo unto the liar, for he shall be thrust down to hell" (2 Nephi 9:34). The honor code is still in force. Neither a dishonest man nor a man lacking in integrity can be saved in the kingdom of God.

PAY YOUR OFFERINGS

The fifth commandment: *Thou shalt pay thy tithes and offerings unto the Lord.*

The commentary: Tithes and offerings divide the faithful from the unfaithful. All men will give an accounting before the judgment bar for the manner in which they used the moneys and properties that came into their hands while in mortality. "The love of money is the root of all evil" (1 Timothy 6:10). And that includes the inordinate attachment to money that is legally and properly your own. The Lord said to Martin Harris, "And again, I command thee that thou shalt not covet thine own property, but impart it freely to the printing of the Book of Mormon" (D&C 19:26). Speaking of making our money and property available for building up the kingdom, Paul says, "He which soweth sparingly shall reap also sparingly; and he which soweth bountifully shall reap also bountifully. Every man according as he purposeth in his heart, so let him give; not grudgingly, or of necessity: for God loveth a cheerful giver" (2 Corinthians 9:6–7). Well might we remember the revelation which says, "For he that is tithed shall not be burned at his coming" (D&C 64:23). Some people say tithing is pretty good fire insurance.

KEEP THE SABBATH

The sixth commandment: *Thou shalt go to sacrament meeting and keep the Sabbath day holy.*

The commentary: We live in an age when almost the whole world is rushing about madly in search of pleasure. Nearly everyone sets the weekend apart for recreational purposes, and this means for Sabbath violation. The generality of mankind fish, play golf, go to movies, or otherwise (as they suppose) seek surcease from the toil of the week. There are churches which conduct their worship services on Friday evening or Saturday morning to free their adherents for recreational pursuits on the Lord's day. The law of the Lord, given anew in our day, counsels us:

That thou mayest more fully keep thyself unspotted from the world, thou shalt go to the house of prayer and offer up thy sacraments upon my holy day;

For verily this is a day appointed unto you to rest from your labors, and to pay thy devotions unto the Most High. [D&C 59:9–10]

KEEP THE WORD OF WISDOM

The seventh commandment: *Thou shalt keep the Word of Wisdom.*

The commentary: We have received from the Lord a law of health, which, if kept, will assure us not only of physical well-being, but also of great outpourings of spiritual enlightenment. This law is divided into affirmative counsel, telling us what we may properly eat, and negative counsel, which forbids the use of certain things which are injurious to the body. While the great hosts of men—of people in the world—reel and stagger through life in an alcoholic stupor; while they immerse themselves in the stinking fumes of tobacco; while they drown themselves in gallons of semipoisonous tea and coffee; while they inhale the smoke of marijuana or otherwise afflict themselves with mind-destroying drugs; the Saints of the Most High, in all their peculiarity, avoid these things for the plague that they are.

Theirs is this promise:

And all saints who remember to keep and do these sayings, walking in obedience to the commandments, shall receive health in their navel and marrow to their bones;

And shall find wisdom and great treasures of knowledge, even hidden treasures;

And shall run and not be weary, and shall walk and not faint.

And I, the Lord, give unto them a promise, that the destroying angel shall pass by them, as the children of Israel, and not slay them. [D&C 89:18–21]

Now note what was involved: First, "walking in obedience to the commandments," for the World of Wisdom is more than a law of health; and second, those keeping it "shall find wisdom and great treasures of knowledge, even hidden treasures." These hidden treasures include such things as a testimony of the truth and divinity of the work, personal revelation to guide us in all our affairs and to provide us with the constant companionship of the Holy Spirit. And the eternal decree is that the Spirit will not dwell in an unclean tabernacle.

BELIEVE TRUE DOCTRINES

The eighth commandment: *Thou shalt believe true doctrines and reject the false educational theories of the world.*

The commentary: We are saved or damned by what we believe. If we believe in the Lord Jesus Christ and the saving truths of his everlasting gospel, we have a hope of eternal life. If our beliefs embrace the philosophies of men and the vagaries of the world, they may lead to destruction. Nearly the whole educational world goes blithely along, espousing the false theories of organic evolution, which rule out the fall of man and the atonement of Christ. Men worship at the shrine of intellectuality without ever realizing that religion is a thing of the Spirit and that "the things of God knoweth no man, but the Spirit of God" (1 Corinthians 2:11). Our schools teach some principles of socialism, of communism, of so-called women's liberation, of curtailing population growth and the like—much of which runs counter to revealed gospel truths.

How grateful we should be for the revealed knowledge we have of the eternal saving truths of the gospel. We know the verities that must be comprehended, understood, and applied to our lives to give us joy and peace in this life and eternal life in the world to come. These things pertain to the nature and kind of being that God is and to the great plan of salvation, which he ordained to enable his spirit children to advance and progress and become like him. The fact that Adam fell, bringing temporal and spiritual death into the world, and the fact that God sent his Only Begotten Son into the world to ransom men from the effects of the temporal and spiritual death brought upon all mankind through the fall of Adam—these are eternal verities. Other eternal verities are these—that God has spoken in our day; that the fulness of his everlasting gospel has been restored; that the church, the kingdom of God, has been set up on earth anew; that it administers the gospel by the power of the holy priesthood; and that there are had among us the gifts, signs, miracles, and all the wonders, blessings, and graces that were ever had in any day when the Lord had a people on earth.

SERVE YOUR FELLOWMEN

The ninth commandment: *Thou shalt serve thy fellowmen and sacrifice for the building up of the kingdom.*

The commentary: Service and sacrifice are essential to salvation. Jesus said, "I am among you as he that serveth" (Luke 22:27). King Benjamin said, "When ye are in the service of your fellow beings ye are only in the service your God" (Mosiah 2:17). Joseph Smith taught that "a religion that does not require the sacrifice of all things, never has power sufficient to produce the faith necessary unto life and salvation" (*Lectures on Faith*, 6:7)

PRAY

The tenth commandment: *Thou shalt pour out thy soul to the Lord in mighty prayer.*

The commentary: We are a praying people—not giving lip service only, not reciting mere words, not repeating memorized phrases—but praying with all the energy and power we possess, praying until the heavens open and the Lord rains down righteousness upon us. No one can pray with perfect faith unless he keeps the commandments. An immoral man can never generate the faith to raise the dead. A person who does not keep the Word of Wisdom will be hindered in healing the sick, and so on right down to the dress and grooming standards.

GOD'S KINGDOM ON EARTH

Such, I suggest, are the ten commandments of a peculiar people. If we live by the principles set forth in them we shall have peace in this life and be inheriters of eternal life in the world to come. If any of us now fall short in any degree, the door is open for repentance. The Lord's arm is not shortened that he will not hear, but he invites all men to come to him and partake of his goodness and grace.

There is an organization in his kingdom whereby we can receive the counsel and direction that we need. All of us have power to set our lives in order to the full so that we do "live soberly, godly, and righteously" in this present world and thereby gain the promised peace and the promised hope of eternal reward. And there is great reward in what we're talking about.

"What are these which are arrayed in white robes? and whence came they?" The inspired answer is "These are they which came out of great tribulation, and have washed their robes, and made them white in the blood of the Lamb" (Revelation 7:13–14). No one ever said or claimed that life was intended to be easy. The Lord deliberately has left us in a situation where the world is all around us and where we have to make the choices. If we choose to follow him and take the counsel that is given, we reap the blessings. And if we choose otherwise, we follow the course that the world follows and the destruction promised to them will be heaped upon us also. "To him that overcometh will I grant to sit with me in my throne, even as I also overcame, and am set down with my father in his throne" (Revelation 3:21). "He that overcometh shall inherit all things; and I will be his god, and he shall be my son" (Revelation 21:7).

What a glorious and wondrous thing it is to be a member of the church and kingdom of God on earth, to have the revelations of heaven, and to know what is meant by the prophetic utterances and the counsels written by prophets and apostles. We are so blessed. This Church of Jesus Christ of Latter-day Saints is God's kingdom on earth. It is led by the spirit of inspiration. If we follow the counsel and direction that we receive, then these principles about which we have talked will live in our lives. They will live because they are true and because the Lord wants to operate by these standards. Out of that kind of a course we shall get the joy and the peace that "passeth all understanding" (Philippians 4:7) while we are here in mortality, and we'll have a guaranteed inheritance of glory, honor, immortality, and exaltation in the realms ahead. Of this I testify and for these things I pray for all of us, in the name of Jesus Christ. Amen.

"Who Shall Declare His Generation?"

Bruce R. McConkie

I have prayed and pondered earnestly to learn what the Lord wants me to say on this occasion. In the early hours of the morning, as I tossed and turned in bed and kept my wife awake, I concluded upon a subject. I shall talk, if I am properly guided by the Spirit, about what I consider in some respects to be the third greatest miracle that has ever occurred in all eternity. This miracle is of such a nature and of such moment that its accomplishment was attended by a heavenly choir, who sang, "Glory to God in the highest, and on earth peace, good will toward men" (Luke 2:14). It was attended by an angelic visitant who proclaimed to all of earth's inhabitants that "unto [us] is born this day in the city of David a Saviour, which is Christ the Lord" (Luke 2:11). It is clear that, if we are to consider this matter, we need a great outpouring of the Holy Spirit. I need it so that what is said may be expressed discreetly and wisely and in harmony with the mind and will of the Lord, and you need it so that the thoughts expressed will sink into your hearts and you will have a feeling of their eternal verity.

This devotional address was given at Brigham Young University on 2 December 1975.

THE THREE GREATEST MIRACLES OF ETERNITY

As I analyze and view the matter, it seems to me that the greatest miracle that ever occurred was the miracle of creation: the fact that God, our Heavenly Father, brought us into being, the fact that we exist; that we were born as his spirit children; and that now we are privileged to abide in mortal tabernacles and partake of a probationary experience.

It seems to me that the second greatest miracle that has ever occurred, in this or any of God's creations, is the atoning sacrifice of his Son; the fact that he came into the world to ransom men from the temporal and spiritual death brought into existence by the fall of Adam; the fact that he is reconciling us again to God and making immortality and eternal life available to us. This atoning sacrifice of Christ is the greatest thing that has even happened since the creation.

You probably know that the Prophet was once asked, "What are the fundamental principles of your religion?" He responded:

The fundamental principles of our religion are the testimony of the Apostles and Prophets, concerning Jesus Christ, that He died, was buried, and rose again the third day, and ascended into heaven; all other things which pertain to our religion are only appendages to it. [*Teachings of the Prophet Joseph Smith*, p. 121]

The very heart and core and center of revealed religion is the atoning sacrifice of Christ. All things rest upon it, all things are operative because of it, and without it there would be nothing. Without it the purposes of creation would be void, they would vanish away, there would be neither immortality nor eternal life, and the ultimate destiny of all men would be to become as Lucifer and his followers are.

The underlying foundation upon which the atoning sacrifice of Christ rests is the doctrine of divine sonship, by which we mean that the Lord Jesus, the firstborn spirit child of the Father, having been foreordained to his mission, was born into this world, on the one hand as the Son of God, inheriting thus from his Father the power of immortality; and that he was born, on the other hand, as the offspring of a mortal women, inheriting from Mary, his mother, the power of mortality. Thus he became the only person who has ever lived who had the power within himself to either live or die as he chose—and therefore the power to work out the infinite and eternal atoning sacrifice upon which all things rest. It seems to me that it would be appropriate on this occasion—as we come into the Christmas period, when we gladly and joyously join with all Christendom in commemorating the traditional day of his birth—for us to talk about the doctrine of his coming into mortality. This is what I consider, in many respects, to be the third greatest miracle of eternity.

MESSIANIC TEXTS IN THE SCRIPTURES

There are several texts that we might take. One text is the great messianic utterance of Isaiah, which he couched in these simple words: "Who shall declare his generation?" (Isaiah 53:8). This means, "Who will give his genesis? Who will reveal his genealogy? Who will give the source from whence he sprang? Who will announce the divinity of the mortal Messiah?" We might also take another text, and this is one that Jesus himself spoke. He said, "Whose son is he?" This is the context: "What think ye of Christ? whose son is he? They say unto him, The Son of David. He saith unto them, How then doth David in spirit call him Lord, saying, The Lord said unto my Lord, Sit thou on my right hand, till I make thine enemies thy footstool?" (Matthew 22:42–44).

Whose son is he? Is he the son of a mortal father and a mortal mother? Is he the Son of God? Is he separate and apart from all mankind by virtue of the birth that was his? Who shall declare his generation? We have an account in the New Testament that begins, "The book of the generation of Jesus Christ" (Matthew 1:1). Then Matthew proceeds to outline what appears to be the ancestry of the Lord, but we can't quite figure out how it fits in with other scriptural passages, at least in the form it has come to us. Luke gives another account that does not agree with that in the book of Matthew. We suppose it may be that one of them is a kingly, royal genealogy, intended to indicate his position and place as the one to sit upon the throne of his father, David; the other is possibly a genealogy either of Mary or Joseph—we can't be sure. The commentaries of the world talk about the virgin birth as being "pious fiction." No one, they say, could have been born that way; it was something which Matthew assumed, and so it became a tradition in the early Church. This matter of genealogy, this matter of the birth of our Lord, is at the heart of Christendom. Thanks be to God that by the opening of the heavens and by revelation in our day we have gained an understanding of what is involved. As a result we can put the atoning sacrifice in its proper position and relationship to all things, and then we are in a position to work out our salvation and do the things that we must do if we are to inherit peace and happiness in this life and go on to eternal glory in the life to come.

Whose son is he? He is the firstborn spirit child of God, our Heavenly Father. There is no possible way to conceive of the genealogy, the genesis, the generation of Christ, without knowing that God our Father is a personal being in whose image we are created; that he has a body of flesh and bones as tangible as man's—the father of the spirits of all men. The Lord Jesus, the great Jehovah, the creator of all things under the Father, is the firstborn of all that spirit host.

In that premortal life our Father ordained and established a plan of salvation named the gospel of God, which plan was to enable his spirit children, Christ included, to advance and progress and become like him. In that day he issued a great cry, a great proclamation went forth through the councils of eternity, with reference to the Father's plan. He said, "Whom shall I send to be my Son, to work out the infinite and eternal atoning sacrifice? Whom shall I send to be born into mortality, inheriting from me the power of immortality? Whom shall I send to lay down his life for the sins of men and to reconcile fallen man to me?" When that great cry went forth, as you know, there were two volunteers. One stepped forward, the firstborn of the Father, the Lord Jesus, and said, "Here am I. Send me. I will be thy son. I will do thy will. I will follow thy plan, do all things in harmony with that which thou hast ordained." There was another volunteer, and he said, "Here am I, send me, I will be thy son, and I will redeem

all mankind, . . . and surely I will do it; wherefore give me thine
honor" (Moses 4:1)—that is, "Let me replace you and be exalted and
most noble of all the persons who live and are." Well, the decree was
issued: "I will send the first" (Abraham 3:27), and that was the day
when there was war in heaven, as you know.

The first volunteer was the Lord Jesus Christ; he then became the
Lamb slain from the foundation of the world, the one appointed to
come down and do all things needed to put in operation his Father's
plan. Now from that day, from the day of creation on, the prophets
foretold his coming and ministry. We call these prophetic utterances messianic prophecies, as for instance, "Behold, a virgin shall
conceive, and bear a son, and shall call his name Immanuel" (Isaiah
7:14). Or "For unto us a child is born, unto us a son is given: and the
government shall be upon his shoulder: and his name shall be called
Wonderful, Counselor, The mighty God, The everlasting Father,
The Prince of Peace. Of the increase of his government and peace
there shall be no end, upon the throne of David, and upon his kingdom, to order it, and to establish it with judgment and with justice
from henceforth even for ever" (Isaiah 9:6–7).

How many sermons were preached in ancient Israel on these
messianic texts we can only imagine. The most perfect prophecies
and the greatest sermons are found in the Book of Mormon. Here is
a sermon-prophecy that an angel spoke to a Nephite prophet:

*For behold, the time cometh, and is not far distant, that with power,
the Lord Omnipotent who reigneth, who was, and is from all eternity to
all eternity, shall come down from heaven among the children of men, and
shall dwell in a tabernacle of clay, and shall go forth amongst men, working
mighty miracles, such as healing the sick, raising the dead, causing the lame
to walk, the blind to receive their sight, and the deaf to hear, and curing all
manner of diseases.*

*And he shall cast out devils, or evil spirits which dwell in the hearts of
the children of men.*

*And lo, he shall suffer temptations, and pain of body, hunger, thirst, and
fatigue, even more than man can suffer, except it be unto death; for behold,*

blood cometh from every pore, so great shall be his anguish for the wickedness and the abominations of his people.

And he shall be called Jesus Christ, the Son of God, the Father of heaven and earth, the Creator of all things from the beginning; and his mother shall be called Mary. [Mosiah 3:5–8]

ACCOUNTS OF THE SAVIOR'S BIRTH

In due course, at the appointed time, in the fulness of the Lord's own time, the Savior was born into the world. Who shall declare his generation? We have attempts made by prophetic writers of old. Matthew says, "Now the birth of Jesus Christ was on this wise: When as his mother Mary was espoused to Joseph, before they came together, she was found with child of the Holy Ghost" (Matthew 1:18). And then he recites what happened and quotes the prophetic utterance of Isaiah about the virgin birth. Let me read you the kindred passage in the book of Luke, this one spoken by Gabriel to Mary:

The angel said unto her, Fear not, Mary: for thou hast found favour with god.

And, behold, thou shalt conceive in thy womb, and bring forth a son, and shalt call his name Jesus.

He shall be great, and shall be called the Son of the Highest; and the Lord God shall give unto him the throne of his father David:

And he shall reign over the house of Jacob for ever; and of his kingdom there shall be no end.

Then said Mary unto the angel, How shall this be, seeing I know not a man?

And the angel answered and said unto her, The Holy Ghost shall come upon thee, and the power of the Highest shall overshadow thee: therefore also that holy thing which shall be born of thee shall be called the Son of God. [Luke 1:30–35]

Now I take those two statements—one written by Matthew and the other by Luke—not perhaps perfectly transcribed and recorded for us in their present form, and I add these words spoken by Alma as the Holy Ghost moved upon him. Alma, as we shall see, will tie together what Matthew and Luke have written and give us the accurate and perfect perspective as to the generation of the Lord Jesus. He said:

> *Repent ye, and prepare the way of the Lord, and walk in his paths, which are straight; for behold, the kingdom of heaven is at hand, and the Son of God cometh upon the face of the earth.*
>
> *And behold, he shall be born of Mary, at Jerusalem which is the land of our forefathers, she being a virgin, a precious and chosen vessel, who shall be overshadowed and conceived by the power of the Holy Ghost, and bring forth a son, yea, even the Son of God.* [Alma 7:9–10]

Now I shall call your attention to one other passage, and then we shall see if we know the answer to our query, "Who shall declare his generation?" This passage is from that wondrous marvelous vision that Nephi had. He said:

> *I beheld the city of Nazareth; and in the city of Nazareth I beheld a virgin, and she was exceedingly fair and white.*
>
> *And it came to pass that I saw the heavens open; and an angel came down and stood before me; and he said unto me: Nephi, what beholdest thou?*
>
> *And I said unto him: A virgin, most beautiful and fair above all other virgins.*
>
> *And he said unto me: Knowest thou the condescension of God?* [If an angel had asked that of you, what would your answer have been? Nephi was a little hesitant. He knew in part, but not in full.]
>
> *And I said unto him: I know that he loveth his children; nevertheless, I do not know the meaning of all things.*
>
> *And he said unto me: Behold, the virgin whom thou seest is the mother of the Son of God, after the manner of the flesh.*
>
> *And it came to pass that I beheld that she was carried away in the Spirit; and after she had been carried away in the Spirit for the space of a time the angel spake unto me again, saying: Look!*
>
> *And I looked and beheld the virgin again, bearing a child in her arms.*

And the angel said unto me: Behold the Lamb of God, yea, even the Son of the Eternal Father! [1 Nephi 11:13–21]

Who shall declare his generation? Whose son is he? Well, now it is perfectly clear. On the one hand he is the Son of God, the God who said in messianic vein, "Thou are my Son; this day have I begotten thee" (Psalms 2:7). On the other hand, he is the son of David and the son of Mary. He inherited from his Father the power of immortality and from his mortal ancestors the power of mortality. How do we know this? How can it be established? We are dealing with spiritual things. Matthew says his book is the book of the generation of Jesus Christ, and he records the facts. He says there was a virgin birth; but the whole world—Christians, so-called—contends and is uncertain and has difficult feelings about this passage. Some say, "Yes, he was born of a virgin," and others say, "It was a pious tradition." Then we read the Book of Mormon account, and we discover what the perfect rendition of the doctrine is. Whose son is he and how do you know? Paul said a very impressive thing: "No man can say that Jesus is the Lord, but by the Holy Ghost" (1 Corinthians 12:3). The Prophet improved this by saying: "No man can know that Jesus is the Lord, but by the Holy Ghost."

TESTIMONY OF THE SAVIOR'S GENEALOGY

Who shall declare his generation? Whose son is he? We have been called out of darkness into the marvelous light of Christ. We have been called to the place where the heavens are opened, where the gifts of the Holy Ghost are poured out bounteously, abundantly, upon all the members of the Church who seek the Lord in integrity and uprightness of heart. We have the gifts of the Spirit, we have the gift of revelation, and we know what is involved in these things. Every member of the Church has had the hands of a legal administrator placed upon his head and the decree issued: "Receive the Holy Ghost." This means that we receive the gift of the Holy Ghost, which is the right to the constant companionship of that member of the Godhead, based on faithfulness.

Who shall declare his generation? His generation can be declared only by living witnesses who have had the revelation of the Holy Ghost, which certifies to their souls that Jesus is the Lord. There is no possible way to know that he is Christ above all, that all power is resident in him, that he is God's Son, except by the process and means of revelation. Peter received a personal revelation as he stood in the presence of the Lord, and it came by the power of the Holy Ghost. He certified, "Thou art the Christ, the Son of the living God" (Matthew 16:16), and received a blessing from the Lord for the witness that he had borne.

Now, if we want to know who is going to declare his generation, the answer is that it is the Latter-day Saints; it is the elders of Israel; it is the prophets and apostles who minister among us; and it is all of those among us who have lived in such a manner that we know by the whisperings of the Holy Ghost to the spirit within us that there is eternal verity, that these things are true. You can be one, as well as I can be one, who declares the generation of Jesus Christ, who gives his genealogy, who comes to know in his heart by a power that is beyond intellectuality that he is the Lord, that God is the Father; and this is the beginning of a course of personal righteousness. Unless and until we know that Jesus is the Lord and that God is his Father, we do not have testimonies of the truth and divinity of the work. In our day a testimony is to know, number one, that Jesus is the Lord, which is the doctrine of the divine sonship. It is to know, number two, that Joseph Smith is a prophet of God and a revealer of the knowledge of Christ and of salvation for us in our day. And it is, number three, to know that The Church of Jesus Christ of Latter-day Saints is the only true and living church upon the face of the whole earth.

Now, I am just one among you. There are thousands of us here congregated in the spirit of worship. I have been speaking and you listening, and the Spirit of the Lord has been present. I have given utterance to truths that are eternal, that will endure to all ages, that are the great foundation upon which the cause of truth and righteousness rests. Those truths have sunk into the hearts of all of you who have been endowed with the same Spirit, and you know as I know that they are true.

Now, in conclusion, I, acting as voice, as mouth as it were for you, declare the generation of the Lord Jesus, his genesis, the source from which he sprang: He is God's son. He was born into this world after the manner of the flesh, with God as his father and Mary as his mother, inheriting the powers of mortality and immortality thereby. He was thus able to work out the infinite and eternal atoning sacrifice. He was thus able to bow in that garden outside Jerusalem's walls, that garden called Gethsemane, and take upon himself the sins of all men on conditions of repentance. That act is the greatest miracle of all time since the miracle of creation, and underlying it is the event which we celebrate with the world this coming season, the birth of our Lord into mortality. Is it any wonder that angelic choir sang, "Glory to God on high, and peace to men"? That is the message we proclaim at this season, and we do it with a sure knowledge whereof we speak, and in the name of the Lord Jesus Christ. Amen.

"Jesus Christ, and Him Crucified"

Bruce R. McConkie

We have assembled here tonight in the spirit of worship and gratitude and thanksgiving, desiring, I think, to be fed the bread of life, to have the guidance and edifying, uplifting influence of the Holy Spirit. We need very much to be so guided. If I can be given utterance and be guided by the power of the Spirit, what I shall say will be what the Lord wants said; it will be what he would say if he personally were here. It will be the mind and will and voice of the Lord and the power of God unto salvation (see D&C 68:4). And if each of you can have that same Spirit resting upon you, then you will have that burning assurance and feeling in your soul that will certify that the truths taught are accurate and right, and that, if we live our lives in conformity to them, we'll be making progress along the path leading to eternal life in our Father's kingdom.

Now, I've left my mind free, hoping that proper inspiration might be given, but I've thought that if I am properly guided, I shall take this sentence that Paul wrote and use it as a theme, or a text. He said, "I determined not to know any thing among you, save Jesus Christ,

This fireside address was given at Brigham Young University on 5 September 1976.

and him crucified" (1 Corinthians 2:2). That, then, is my subject: Jesus Christ, and him crucified.

To set the stage and lay a foundation for what appropriately might be said about this subject, I shall read three quotations. One is from the Doctrine and Covenants; in it the Lord says:

Learn of me, and listen to my words; walk in the meekness of my Spirit, and you shall have peace in me. [D&C 19:23]

The second, Nephi writing, is from the Book of Mormon:

Believe in Christ, and . . . be reconciled to God; for we know that it is by grace that we are saved, after all we can do. . . .

And we talk of Christ, we rejoice in Christ, we preach of Christ, we prophesy of Christ, and we write according to our prophecies, that our children may look for a remission of their sins. . . .

. . . Believe in Christ, and deny him not; and Christ is the Holy One of Israel; wherefore ye must bow down before him, and worship him with all your might, mind, and strength, and your whole soul; and if ye do this ye shall in nowise be cast out. [2 Nephi 25:23, 26, 29]

The third quotation, from the Prophet Joseph Smith, gives us information that he learned by translating the papyrus, a portion of which is published as the book of Abraham:

Everlasting covenant was made between three personages before the organization of this earth, and relates to their dispensation of things to men on the earth; these personages, according to Abraham's record, are called: God the first, the Creator; God the second, the Redeemer; and God the third, the Witness or Testator. [*Teachings of the Prophet Joseph Smith*, p. 190]

Now, we are members of The Church of Jesus Christ of Latter-day Saints. We have taken upon ourselves his name in the waters of baptism. We renew the covenant therein made when we partake of the sacrament. If we have been born again, we have become the sons and daughters of the Lord Jesus Christ. We are members of his family. We are obligated and expected to live by the standards of the family. Because of that family membership, that close association, we have the privilege of an intimate association with him. We have been given the gift of the Holy Ghost, which is the constant companionship of that member of the Godhead based on faithfulness. And that Holy Spirit has as one of his chief missions to bear record of the Father and the Son and to reveal to us, in a way that cannot be controverted or questioned, his divine sonship and the glorious truths that are in him.

Salvation is in Christ. We have set ourselves apart from the generality of mankind and have become his witnesses. And so tonight, if we may be properly guided, and have all our thoughts and attentions centered on this matter, so that we will be mutually edified, I shall call attention to some of the great, basic realities in the eternal scheme of things. And as we shall see, all of these things, as far as we are now concerned, center in the Lord Jesus Christ.

TRUTH AND HERESY ABOUT THE GODHEAD

Now, to begin with, we start with God, our Heavenly Father, who is here named God the first, the Creator. And we have to understand that he is a holy and perfected and exalted person; that he is a being in whose image man is created; that he has a body of flesh and bones as tangible as man's; and that we are literally his spirit children, the Lord Jesus being the firstborn. I suggest that the greatest truth in all eternity, bar none, is that there is a God in heaven who is a personal being, in whose image man is made, and that we are his spirit children. We must build on that rock foundation before any progression ever begins in the spiritual realm. We first believe in God our Heavenly Father.

I suggest also that the greatest heresy that was ever devised by an evil power was the heresy that defines the nature and kind of being that God is as a spirit essence that fills immensity; as a being without body, parts, or passions; as something that is incomprehensible, uncreated, and unknowable. The greatest truth is God; the greatest

heresy is the doctrine that recites the opposite of the truth as to
God's person.

I suggest that the second greatest truth in all eternity is that
Christ our Lord is the Redeemer; that he was foreordained in the
councils of eternity to come down here and work out the infinite and
eternal atoning sacrifice; that because of what he did we are ransomed
from the effects of the temporal and spiritual death that came into
the world by the fall of Adam. Because of what he did, all of us gain
immortality, meaning that we shall come forth in the resurrection.
And all of us have the hope, the potential, the possibility, to gain
eternal life in addition to immortality, meaning that we can become
like God our Heavenly Father. That is the second greatest truth in
all eternity.

The second greatest heresy in all eternity is the doctrine that
denies the divine sonship, that sets up a system that says you can give
lip-service to the name of Christ, but you are saved by grace alone
without efforts and without work on your part.

Now I suggest, conformable to what the Prophet said about God
the third, who is the Witness or Testator, that the third greatest truth
in all eternity is that the Holy Spirit of God, a personage of spirit,
a member of the Godhead, has power to reveal eternal truth to the
heart and soul and mind of man. And that revelation—known first
as a testimony, and then known as the general receipt of truth in the
spiritual field—that testimony is the great thing that man needs to
lead him on a course back to our Father in Heaven.

Since that is the third greatest truth in all eternity, it follows
that the third greatest and most serious heresy in all eternity is the
doctrine that denies that the Holy Spirit of God reveals truth to the
human soul and that denies that there are gifts of the spirit, that there
are miracles and powers and graces and good things that the Lord by
his Spirit pours out upon mortal men.

We ought to have in our hearts an overflowing feeling of
gratitude and thanksgiving. We praise the Lord our God, meaning the Father, because he created us. If he had not created us, we
would not be; neither would the earth, or the sidereal heavens, or the

universe, or anything else. If there had been no eternal God and no creation, there would be nothing. And because we exist, we ought in our souls to have an infinite degree of gratitude and thanksgiving to God our Heavenly Father.

Now, secondly, we ought to have an infinite degree of gratitude and thanksgiving to Christ the Lord, because he worked out the infinite and eternal atoning sacrifice and put into operation the terms and conditions of the Father's plan. If there had been no atonement of Christ, there would be no resurrection. And if there had been no atonement of Christ, there would be no eternal life, and hence our bodies would have lain forever in the dust and our spirits everlastingly been cast out from the presence of God, and we would have become like the devil and his angels (see 2 Nephi 9:7–9). What I am saying is that, through the atoning sacrifice of the Lord Jesus, the plan of the Father became operative. Its terms and conditions were put into force; they were given efficacy and validity. And so we ought to rejoice and have thanksgiving and gratitude in our souls to the Lord Jesus, who redeemed us.

Now, thirdly, by virtue of obedience to the laws that are ordained and by becoming clean and spotless and pure, because the Spirit will not dwell in an unclean tabernacle, we get in a position to receive revelation by the power of the Holy Spirit. Once we are in tune, then we become part of the family of the Lord Jesus. We partake of the same spirit that he possesses; we begin to believe as he believed, to act as he acted, to speak as he spoke. As a consequence, we get in a position to gain that glory and eternal life which he, as our prototype, has already gained. And so, thirdly, we rejoice in what has come to us by the power of the Holy Ghost and have, again, an infinite gratitude where those things are concerned.

THE PLAN OF SALVATION

God our Heavenly Father ordained and established the plan of salvation. Joseph Smith expressed it in these words. He said, "God himself, finding he was in the midst of spirits and glory, because he was more intelligent, saw proper to institute laws whereby the rest could have a privilege to advance like himself" (*Teachings of the Prophet Joseph Smith*, p. 354). God is exalted and omnipotent and enthroned; he has all power, all might, and all dominion. He lives in the family unit, and the name of the kind of life that he lives is eternal life. And so if we advance and progress and go forward until we become like him, we then become, like Christ, inheritors of eternal life in the kingdom of God. That is our aim and our goal. Hence there is this thing which Paul calls "the gospel of God," meaning that the Father ordained and established the plan of salvation. But then Paul says, "Concerning his Son Jesus Christ our Lord, which was made of the seed of David according to the flesh" (Romans 1:2–3), meaning that Christ adopted the Father's plan. He made it his own. He espoused it. He became the advocate of salvation, the leader in the cause of salvation—all because he was chosen to be born into the world as God's Son.

All of this was known and taught and understood in the great eternities that went before. We all heard the gospel preached. We knew its terms and conditions. We knew what would be involved in this mortal probation. We knew that it was necessary to come here and get a mortal body as a step toward gaining an immortal body, one of flesh and bones. We knew that when we came here we would need to be tried and examined and tested. We'd need to undergo probationary experiences when we were outside the presence of God, when we walked by faith rather than by sight, when the spirit was housed in a tabernacle of clay and subject to the lusts and appetites and passions of mortality. This we all knew. And then our Father sent forth the great decree through the councils of eternity, "Whom shall I send to be my son, to work out the infinite and eternal atoning sacrifice, to be born into mortality with the power of immortality, to inherit from me the power to work out the infinite and eternal atoning sacrifice?" He got two volunteers. Christ the Lord said, "Father, thy will be done" (see Moses 4:1–3). That is, "I will go down and do what thou hast ordained and sacrifice myself. I will be the lamb slain from the foundation of the world" (see Moses 7:47). Lucifer wanted to modify the Father's plan so radically that we could almost say he offered a new system of salvation. He wanted to deny all men their agency, to save all men, and, in return, to receive the power and dignity and glory of the Father. He wanted to take the place of the Father. The decision was then made: "I will send the first" (Abraham 3:27).

The plan was put into operation. Part of it was the creation of this earth. Then came its peopling. We are all the sons and daughters of Father Adam; all of us are eternal beings, offspring of Deity. Our mortal bodies have been made from the dust of the earth. We're here, having mortal bodies, being examined and tried and tested to see if we will walk uprightly and keep the commandments.

Now, our first obligation is to believe in Christ and accept him literally and completely and fully for what he is. We believe in Christ when we believe the doctrine he teaches, the words that he speaks, the message that he proclaims. When he came in the flesh as Mary's son, the account says that he "went about . . . preaching the gospel of the kingdom" (Matthew 9:35), meaning that his message was a revelation to people in that day of the plan of salvation, of the things that they had to do to overcome the world, to perfect their lives, and to qualify to go back with him to the presence of the everlasting Father.

So, first of all, we believe in Christ. And the test as to whether we believe in him is whether we believe his words and whether we believe those whom he hath sent—the apostles and prophets of all the ages. And then, having believed, we have the obligation of conforming to the truths that we have thus learned. If we do conform we begin to grow in spiritual graces. We add to our faith virtue, and to virtue knowledge, and to knowledge temperance and patience and godliness and all of the other attributes and characteristics that are written in the revelations (see 2 Peter 1:5–7). So step by step and degree by degree we begin to become like God our Heavenly Father.

We do not work out our salvation in a moment; it doesn't come to us in an instant, suddenly. Gaining salvation is a process. Paul says, "Work out your own salvation with fear and trembling" (Philippians 2:12). To some members of the Church who had been baptized and who were on the course leading to eternal life, he said, "Now is our salvation nearer than when we believed" (Romans 13:11). That is, "We have made some progress along the straight and narrow path.

We are going forward, and if we continue in that direction, eternal life will be our everlasting reward."

We start out in the direction of eternal life when we join The Church of Jesus Christ of Latter-day Saints. We enter in at a gate, and the name of the gate is repentance and baptism. We thereby get on a path, and the name of the path is the straight and narrow path. And then if we endure to the end, meaning if we keep the commandments of God after baptism, we go up that straight and narrow path, and at its end is a reward that is named eternal life. All of this is available because of the atoning sacrifice of Christ. If he had not come, there would be no hope, or no possibility under any circumstance, for any man either to be resurrected or to have eternal life. Salvation comes by the mercy and the love and the condescension of God. In other words, it comes by the grace of God, meaning that our Lord made it available. But he has done his work, and we must now do ours; and we have the obligation to endure to the end, to keep the commandments, to work out our salvation, and that is what we are in the process of doing in the Church and the kingdom of God on earth.

THE PROCESS OF ACHIEVING ETERNAL LIFE

We say that a man has to be born again, meaning that he has to die as pertaining to the unrighteous things in the world. Paul said in effect, "Crucify the old man of sin and come forth in a newness of life" (see Romans 6:6). We are born again when we die as pertaining to unrighteousness and when we live as pertaining to the things of the Spirit. But that doesn't happen in an instant, suddenly. That also is a process. Being born again is a gradual thing, except in a few isolated instances that are so miraculous they get written up in the scriptures. As far as the generality of the members of the Church are concerned, we are born again by degrees, and we are born again to added light and added knowledge and added desires for righteousness as we keep the commandments.

The same thing is true of being sanctified. Those who go to the celestial kingdom of heaven have to be sanctified, meaning that they become clean and pure and spotless. They've had evil and sin and iniquity burned out of their souls as though by fire, and the figurative expression there is "the baptism of fire" (see 2 Nephi 31:13–14). Here again it is a *process.* Nobody is sanctified in an instant, suddenly. But if we keep the commandments and press forward with steadfastness after baptism, then degree by degree and step by step we sanctify our souls until that glorious day when we're qualified to go where God and angels are.

So it is with the plan of salvation. We have to become perfect to be saved in the celestial kingdom. But nobody becomes perfect in this life. Only the Lord Jesus attained that state, and he had an advantage that none of us has. He was the Son of God, and he came into this life with a spiritual capacity and a talent and an inheritance that exceeded beyond all comprehension what any of the rest of us was born with. Our revelations say that he was like unto God in the pre-mortal life and he was, under the Father, the creator of worlds without number. That Holy Being was the Holy One of Israel anciently and he was the Sinless One in mortality. He lived a perfect life, and he set an ideal example. This shows that we can strive and go forward toward that goal, but no other mortal—not the greatest prophets nor the mightiest apostles nor any of the righteous saints of any of the ages—has ever been perfect, but we must become perfect to gain a celestial inheritance. As it is with being born again, and as it is with sanctifying our souls, so becoming perfect in Christ is a process.

We begin to keep the commandments today, and we keep more of them tomorrow, and we go from grace to grace, up the steps of the ladder, and we thus improve and perfect our souls. We can become perfect in some minor things. We can be perfect in the payment of tithing. If we pay one-tenth of our interest annually into the tithing funds of the Church, if we do it year in and year out, if we desire to do it and have no intent to withhold, and if we would do it regardless of what arose in our lives, then in that thing we are perfect. And in that thing and to that extent we are living the law as well as Moroni or the angels from heaven could live it. And so degree by degree and step by step we start out on the course to perfection with the objec-

tive of becoming perfect as God our Heavenly Father is perfect, in
which eventuality we become inheritors of eternal life in his kingdom.

As members of the Church, if we chart a course leading to eternal
life; if we begin the processes of spiritual rebirth, and are going in
the right direction; if we chart a course of sanctifying our souls,
and degree by degree are going in that direction; and if we chart a
course of becoming perfect, and, step by step and phase by phase, are
perfecting our souls by overcoming the world, then it is absolutely
guaranteed—there is no question whatever about it—we shall gain
eternal life. Even though we have spiritual rebirth ahead of us, perfection ahead of us, the full degree of sanctification ahead of us, if we
chart a course and follow it to the best of our ability in this life, then
when we go out of this life we'll continue in exactly that same course.
We'll no longer be subject to the passions and the appetites of the
flesh. We will have passed successfully the tests of this mortal probation and in due course we'll get the fulness of our Father's kingdom—
and that means eternal life in his everlasting presence.

The Prophet told us that there are many things that people have
to do, even after the grave, to work out their salvation. We're not
going to be perfect the minute we die. But if we've charted a course,
if our desires are right, if our appetites are curtailed and bridled,
and if we believe in the Lord and are doing to the very best of our
abilities what we ought to do, we'll go on to everlasting salvation,
which is the fulness of eternal reward in our Father's kingdom.

HOPE AND REJOICING

I think we ought to have hope; I think we ought to have rejoicing.
We can talk about the principles of salvation and say how many
there are and how people have to meet these standards. And it may
thereby seem hard and difficult and beyond the capacity of mortals
so to obtain. But we need not take that approach. We ought to real-
ize that we have the same appetites and passions that all of the saints
and righteous people had in the dispensations that have gone before.
They were no different than we are. They overcame the flesh. They
gained the knowledge of God. They understood about Christ and

salvation. They had the revelations of the Holy Spirit to their souls certifying of the divine sonship and of the prophetic ministry of whatever prophets ministered among them. And as a consequence they worked out their salvation.

Occasionally in the overall perspective someone came along who so lived that he was translated, but that's not particularly for our day and generation. When we die our obligation is to go into the spirit world and continue to preach the gospel there. So, as far as people now living are concerned, our obligation is to believe the truth, and live the truth, and chart a course to eternal life. And if we do it, we get peace and joy and happiness in this life, and, when we go into the eternal realms ahead, we continue there to work in the cause of righteousness. And we will not fail! We will go on to eternal reward.

The Prophet Joseph Smith said that no man can commit the unpardonable sin after he departs this life. Of course he can't; that's part of the testing of this mortal probation. And on that same basis, anybody who is living uprightly and has integrity and devotion, if he's doing all that he can here, then when he leaves this sphere he's going to go into the paradise of God and have rest and peace—that is, rest and peace as far as the troubles and turmoils and vicissitudes and anxieties of this life are concerned. But he'll continue to labor and work on the Lord's errand, and eventually he'll come up in the Resurrection of the Just. He'll get an immortal body, meaning that body and spirit will be inseparably connected. That soul will never again see corruption. Never again will there be death, but what is equally as glorious, or more so, that soul will go on to eternal life in the kingdom of God. And eternal life means the continuation of the family unit. Eternal life means inheriting, receiving, and possessing the fulness of the Father, the power and might and creative ability and all that he has that enabled him to create worlds without number and to be the progenitor of an infinite number of spirit progeny.

Now, we can't really conceive of how glorious and wondrous all these things are. We can get some glimmering; we can get a little understanding. We know that they are available because God the Creator established the plan of salvation. We know that they are available because God the Redeemer put into force and gave efficacy and validity to all of the terms and conditions of that eternal plan. And we know that they can be revealed and known to us because God the Witness or Testator bears witness, certifies, testifies to the spirit that is within us in a way that cannot be controverted that the things of which we speak are true.

THE CRUCIFIXION

Now I should like to speak of Jesus Christ, and him crucified, of the atonement of the Lord. The Atonement was worked out in a garden outside Jerusalem's walls, a garden called Gethsemane. It was worked out in a way that is totally beyond our comprehension. We do not understand how. We know some of the why. We know that it did occur. We know that, in a way incomprehensible to a finite intellect, the Son of God took upon himself the sins of all men on conditions of repentance. That is, he paid the penalty. He satisfied the demands of justice. He made mercy available to us. Mercy cometh because of the Atonement. Mercy is for the penitent. Mercy is for the repentant. Everyone else has to suffer for his own sins and pay to the full extent the demands of justice. But our eternal Redeemer, and blessed be his name, has done for us what no one else could, and he did it because he was God's Son and because he possessed the power of immortality. He has taken our sins upon him on conditions of repentance. Repentance means that we have faith in the Lord Jesus Christ, that we forsake our sins, that we come into the Church and kingdom of God on earth and receive the Holy Ghost. Repentance is far more than reformation. Repentance is a gift of God, and it comes to faithful members of the Church. We get it by the power of the Holy Ghost.

The cleansing process that occurs in our lives comes because we receive the cleansing power of the Holy Ghost. The Holy Ghost is a revelator, and the Holy Ghost is a sanctifier. The Holy Ghost reveals truth to every human soul that obeys the law. Obedience qualifies us to know the truth. And then the Holy Ghost sanctifies the human soul, so that we become clean and spotless and eventually are qualified to go where God and Christ are.

GRATITUDE AND THANKSGIVING

Now I say, as we turn our attentions and our thoughts to these infinitely great and wondrous and glorious eternal truths, that we ought to have in our souls gratitude and adoration and thanksgiving, beyond any measure of comprehension, to God our Father, who created us; to Christ our Lord, who redeemed us; and to the Holy Spirit of God, by whose instrumentality we come to know of the truth and verity of these eternal principles upon which salvation rests.

I've recited these principles, or at least I have talked about them. I haven't taken occasion to read any revelations. We could do that, but it doesn't seem needed or appropriate under the circumstances. Let me just suggest to you that the doctrine I have taught and the explanations I have made are scriptural and they are true.

I can bear witness of their truth and verity because I know by the power of the Holy Spirit what is involved. And if the Spirit has been poured out upon you, as I think it has upon many of you, then you also know by the power of that Spirit of the truth and verity of the things about which we are now speaking. And since you know them, then light and truth and knowledge have come into your soul and you have an obligation not only to believe, but also to conform your life to the things that you believe and thereby to chart the glorious and wondrous course leading to eternal life.

I bear record and testimony that what we have been teaching here is true; we are obligated to bear testimony whenever we speak by the power of the Spirit. I say in plain, simple, unambiguous words that the Lord Jesus is the Son of the living God; that he came into the world to be lifted up upon the cross and to be crucified for the sins of the world; that he was born with the power of immortality on the one hand and the power of mortality on the other; and that thereby he voluntarily laid down his life and then took it up again and in some way (incomprehensible to us) worked out the infinite and eternal atoning sacrifice. These things are true!

What a wondrous thing it is to be members of a church and kingdom established by God himself, where these truths are known and understood and taught. I came in here tonight and looked at this wonderful student body, some twenty-four thousand of you assembled for this devotional service, and I thought to myself about what the voice of God spoke to Moses out of the burning bush. He said, "Put off thy shoes from off thy feet, for the place whereon thou standest is holy ground" (Exodus 3:5).

We just happen to be members of God's true Church, and we have apostles and prophets and living oracles to teach and bear record of the truth. We also have elders and witnesses almost without number to reveal and explain these things to us. We are walking where the prophets of God have walked. We go to school at an institution that is guided by the spirit of inspiration, where the hand of the Lord is involved. And if we might paraphrase what his voice said to Moses, we might well say for all of us, with reference to our labors and works at this great institution, "Put off thy shoes from off thy feet, for the place whereon thou walkest is holy ground."

The Lord's hand is in this work. He wants us to be saved. He is pleading with us to keep the commandments. We are in an environment and a climate and living under circumstances where we have every opportunity so to do. And the most glorious, wondrous thing about this whole system of revealed religion is that it is true. You ponder that in your heart. There is nothing connected with our whole system of revealed religion to compare with the simple, pure, unadulterated fact that it's true. And because it's true, it will save a human soul. Because it's true, it will prevail. In due course the knowledge of God will cover the earth as the waters cover the sea. God grant us the insight to live in harmony with the truth. God grant us the revelations of his Holy Spirit so that with one voice we may testify of the truth and renew our determinations to live in harmony with it. And I testify of this truth in the name of the Lord Jesus Christ. Amen.

Celestial Marriage

————◆————

Bruce R. McConkie

I stand before you tonight in the spirit of this musical number, "I Need Thee Every Hour," and hope and pray and desire that I may be given utterance by the power of the Spirit so that I may say those things that will please the Lord, that will be the things he would say if he personally were addressing this great congregation at this hour. When I consulted with Brother Lorin Wheelwright, he told me that it would be most appropriate if I spoke on a Thanksgiving theme, since it would fit in well with the music. I decided to do that, prepared my mind and an outline, and gathered some quotations, but since arriving here tonight I have had nothing but a stupor of thought, nothing but uncertainty in my mind as to that subject. Rather, I think, if I may be guided by the power of the Spirit and say what will please the Lord, I shall talk to you—somewhat informally, perhaps—about the obligation that rests upon Latter-day Saints to create for themselves eternal family units patterned after the family of God, our Heavenly Father.

This fireside address was given at Brigham Young University on 6 November 1977.

So that we may all be united in our thinking and be in a position to build on the same foundation, having in mind the same eternal truths, I shall initially read three or four brief passages from the revelations. I hope and pray that I may be given utterance by the Spirit and that your hearts may be opened by the power of the same Spirit so that we will be mutually edified. I pray that we will be one in feeling and in attitude, where these great doctrinal principles are concerned, and will have riveted in our souls the determination to do all the things that must be done in this mortal probation to inherit the fulness of the glory of our Father's kingdom.

I take for one text these words from Section 42, the revelation entitled "The Law of the Church": "Thou shalt love thy wife with all thy heart, and shalt cleave unto her and none else" (D&C 42:22). And in the spirit of those words, I take from the Old Testament book of Ruth these expressions which, though not originally uttered with reference to marriage, contain a principle that is wholly applicable.

> *And Ruth said, Intreat me not to leave thee, or to return from following after thee: for whither thou goest, I will go; and where thou lodgest, I will lodge: thy people shall be my people, and thy God my God:*
> *Where thou diest, will I die, and there will I be buried: the Lord do so to me, and more also* [and now I will change it slightly], *if* [even] *death part thee and me.* [Ruth 1:16–17]

Now a passage from Section 49 in the Doctrine and Covenants summarizing the basic administrative announcement relative to marriage for our dispensation:

> *Verily I say unto you,* [saith the Lord,] *that whoso forbiddeth to marry is not ordained of God, for marriage is ordained of God unto man.*
> *Wherefore, it is lawful that he should have one wife, and they twain shall be one flesh, and all this that the earth might answer the end of its creation;*
> *And that it might be filled with the measure of man, according to his creation before the world was made.* [D&C 49:15–17]

When we as Latter-day Saints talk about marriage we are talking about a holy celestial order. We are talking about a system out of which can grow the greatest love, joy, peace, happiness, and serenity known to humankind. We are talking about creating a family unit that has the potential of being everlasting and eternal, a family unit where a man and a wife can go on in that relationship to all eternity and where mother and daughter and father and son are bound by eternal ties that will never be severed. We are talking about creating a unit more important than the Church, more important than any organization that exists on earth or in heaven, a unit out of which exaltation and eternal life grow; and when we talk about eternal life, we are talking about the kind of life that God our Heavenly Father lives.

In this final glorious dispensation we have received the most basic truth of all eternity, and that truth concerns the nature and kind of being that God is. It is eternal life to know the Father and the Son (see John 17:3). There is no possible way to go degree by degree, step by step to the high exaltation we seek unless and until we come to a knowledge of the nature and kind of being that God is. Thus, when we talk about eternal life, we are talking about the kind of life that God our Father lives; and when we speak of him, we are speaking of a holy, perfected, exalted, ennobled man—an individual, a personage, a being with "a body of flesh and bones as tangible as man's" (D&C 130:22). We are talking about someone who is a literal parent, who is the Father of the spirits of all men. You and I were born as members of his family. We have seen his face; we have heard his voice; we have received his counsel, personally as well as through representatives and agents; we knew him in the preexistence. Now a curtain has been dropped and we do not have the remembrance that we had then, but we are seeking to do the things that will enable us to be like him.

After he had begotten us as his spirit children, he gave us our agency, which is the power and ability to choose; he also gave us laws and allowed us to obey or disobey, in consequence of which we can and did develop talents, abilities, aptitudes, and characteristics of diverse sorts. He ordained and established a plan of salvation. It was named the gospel of God, meaning God our Heavenly Father, and it consisted of all of the laws, powers, and rights, all of the experiences, all of the gifts and graces needed to take us, his spirit sons and daughters, from our then-spirit state of low intelligence to the high, exalted state where we would be like him.

The Prophet Joseph Smith tells us that "God himself, finding he was in the midst of spirits and glory," ordained laws whereby they might advance and progress and become like him (*Teachings of the Prophet Joseph Smith*, p. 354). Those laws included the creation of this earth; they included the receipt of a mortal body where we could be tried and tested in a probationary state and receive experiences impossible to gain in any other way; they included the opportunity to choose between right and wrong, to do good or to do evil, the opportunity to grow and advance in the things of the spirit; and they included the opportunity to enter into a marriage relationship that has the potential of being eternal. We started out on this course in the premortal life. Now we are down here taking the final examination for all the life that we lived back then, which also is the entrance examination for the realms and kingdoms that are ahead.

The name of the kind of life that God our Father lives is eternal life, and eternal life consists of two things: the continuation of the family unit in eternity; and an inheritance of what the scriptures denominate the fulness of the father or the fulness of the glory of the Father (see D&C 76:56), meaning the might, power, dominion, and exaltation that he himself possesses. In our finite circumstances we have no ability or power to comprehend the might and omnipotence of the Father. We can look at the stars in the heavens, we can view the Milky Way, we can see all the worlds and orbs that have been created in their spheres, we can examine all the life on this planet with which we are familiar, and by doing this we can begin to get a concept of the glorious, infinite, unlimited intelligence by which all these things are—and all these things taken together and more dramatize the fulness of the glory of the Father.

We are seeking eternal life—that is to say, we have been offered the privilege to go forward in advancement, as the children of God, until we become like our eternal Parent; and if we so attain it is required, it is requisite, it is mandatory for us to build on the foundation of the atoning sacrifice of the Lord Jesus. It is required of us that we keep the commandments and sow the seeds of righteousness in order to reap the harvest of glory and honor. If we do all the things that the gospel requires of us we can make that kind of advancement. The gospel, which is the plan of salvation, is now named the gospel of Jesus Christ to honor him who worked out the infinite and eternal atoning sacrifice and put into operation all the terms and conditions of the Father's plan.

God our Father is the Creator of all things, and we glorify his holy name and sing praises to him because he created us and, in the ultimate sense, the universe, the earth, and all things on all the orbs in all the sidereal heavens. God our Father is the ultimate and perfect Creator. Jesus Christ, his Son, is the Redeemer. He came to ransom us from the temporal and spiritual death brought into the world by the fall of Adam. The ransom from temporal death gives each of us immortality: "As in Adam all die, even so in Christ shall all be made alive" (1 Corinthians 15:22). And every living soul will rise in the resurrection with immortality and, having so arisen, will be judged according to his works and will be assigned a place in the kingdoms that are prepared. Some will be raised in immortality and then unto eternal life, and eternal life is the name of the kind of life that God lives.

We cannot shout praises to the name of the Lord Jehovah, who is the Lord Jesus, to the extent that we should in order to honor him properly for all that he has done for us and for the possibilities that lie ahead because he took upon himself our sins on conditions of repentance. The work of God the Father was creation, and the work of Christ the Son was redemption. We are men, and our work— building on the foundation that God our Father laid and that Christ his Son has established—is to do the part assigned to us in order to inherit the glory and honor and dignity of which I speak. In general terms, that means that we are to accept and believe the law. We are to believe in Christ and live his law, be upright and clean, have our sins washed away in the waters of baptism, become new creatures by the power of the Holy Ghost, and walk in paths of truth and righteousness.

As long as we speak in this vein, all that we say is said in generalities; it is a foundation for a specific and particular thing toward which we point: eternal marriage. Everything that we do in the Church is connected and associated with and tied into the eternal order of matrimony that God has ordained. Everything that we do from the time that we become accountable through all our experiences and all the counsel and direction we receive up to the time of marriage is designed and intended to prepare us to enter into a probationary marriage arrangement, one that does in fact become eternal if we abide in the covenant made in connection with that order of matrimony. Then everything that we do for the remainder of our lives, whatsoever it may be, ties back into the celestial order of matrimony into which we have entered and is designed and intended to encourage us to keep the covenant made in holy places. That is the general concept, briefly stated, under which we are operating.

Let me now read from the revelation on marriage the general concept governing marriage and everything else. I read from the Doctrine and Covenants, section 132, verse 5: "All who will have a blessing at my hands shall abide the law which was appointed for that blessing, and the conditions thereof, as were instituted from before the foundation of the world." That is the basic, governing, overriding principle that rules all of the acts of men in all ages. No one ever gets anything for nothing. We have received as a free gift the fact of resurrection, but in a sense even that is not free in that we lived meritoriously and uprightly in the pre-existence and earned the right to undergo this mortal probation and the resurrection that follows it. In the broadest and most eternal perspective that there is, no one ever gets anything for nothing; and so we live the law and we get the blessing. And having said that, then the Lord says: "As pertaining to the new and everlasting covenant, it was instituted for the fulness of my glory; and he that receiveth a fulness thereof must and shall abide the law, or he shall be damned, saith the Lord God" (D&C 132:6).

"The new and everlasting covenant" is the fulness of the gospel, and the gospel is the covenant of salvation that the Lord makes with men. It is new because it has been revealed anew in our day; it is everlasting because it has always been had by faithful people, not only on this earth but on all the earths inhabited by the children of our Father. This next verse, number seven, is a one-sentence summary of the whole law of the whole gospel. Of necessity, it is written in legal language because it outlines the terms and conditions that are involved; and of course it is the Lord speaking:

And verily I say unto you, that the conditions of this law are these [this recites the conditions of the law that govern in the whole field of revealed religion, but we will make specific application of it to our central responsibility, which is marriage]: *All covenants, contracts, bonds, obligations, oaths, vows, performances, connections, associations, or expectations, that are not made and entered into and sealed by the Holy Spirit of promise, of him who is anointed, both as well for time and for all eternity, and that too most holy, by revelation and commandment through the medium of mine anointed, whom I have appointed on the earth to hold this power (and I have appointed unto my servant Joseph to hold this power in the last days, and there is never but one on the earth at a time on whom this power and the keys of this priesthood are conferred), are of no efficacy, virtue, or force in and after the resurrection from the dead; for all contracts that are not made unto this end have an end when men are dead.*

Now, what is involved? We have power, as mortals, to make between ourselves any arrangements that we choose to make and that are legal in the society where we live, and they will bind us as long as we agree to be bound, even until death takes us. But we do not have power, as mortals, to bind ourselves after death. Neither you nor I can enter a contract to buy or sell or go or come or paint or perform or do any act in the sphere that is ahead. God has given us our agency here and now as pertaining to mortality.

We are mortal; this is a temporal sphere, a time-bound sphere. And if we are going to do anything here and now that bridges the gulf of death, anything that endures in the spirit world, anything that remains with us in the resurrection, we have to do it by a power that is beyond the power of man—it has to be the power of God. Man is mortal and his acts are limited to mortality; God is eternal and his acts have no end.

The Lord conferred upon Peter the keys of the kingdom of God so that he had power to bind on earth and seal everlastingly in the heavens, and then he spread that out to James and John and then to all of the Twelve anciently so that they all had the same power. In our day he has restored again what was had anciently. He has called apostles and prophets and given them the keys of the kingdom of God, and they have power once again to bind on earth and have it sealed everlastingly in the heavens. He sent Elijah to bring the sealing power; he sent Elias to confer upon Joseph Smith and Oliver Cowdery the gospel of Abraham and to give the promise that in them and in their seed all generations after should be blessed.

Elijah came and Elias came, acting in the power and authority of the Almighty, and gave once again their keys, powers, prerogatives, and rights to mortal men on earth—praise God for this glorious thing! Once again on earth there are people who can bind on earth and have it sealed everlastingly in the heavens. We have the power to perform a marriage, and we can do it so that the man and the woman become husband and wife here and now and—if they keep the covenant there and then made—they will remain husband and wife in the spirit world and will come up in glory and dominion with kingdoms and exaltation in the resurrection, being husband and wife and having eternal life. And it operates thus because in this church, and in this church only, the Lord Almighty has given the sealing power. That is our potential; that is within our possible realm of achievement.

In this one-sentence summary, as I express it, of the whole law of the gospel, we read three requisites. If, for instance, a person is going to have a baptism that lasts eternally he must first find the right baptism; second, find a legal administrator to perform the ordinance for him; and third, have that ordinance sealed by the power of the Holy Spirit, in which event the baptism will admit the repentant person to a celestial heaven in the realms ahead. This matter of being sealed by the Holy Spirit of promise applies to every ordinance and every covenant and all things that there are in the Church. Do not talk about marriage and the Holy Spirit of promise unless and until you understand first the concept and the principle and its universal application.

One of our revelations speaks of "the Holy Spirit of promise, which the Father sheds forth upon all those who are just and true" (D&C 76:53), meaning that every person who walks uprightly, does the best that he can, overcomes the world, rises above carnality, and walks in paths of righteousness will have his acts and his deeds sealed and approved by the Holy Spirit. He will be, as Paul would have expressed it, "justified . . . by the Spirit" (1 Corinthians 6:11). Therefore, if a man is going to be married and wants a marriage that lasts for a week, or three weeks, or three months, or as long as Hollywood prescribes, or even "until death us do part," he can be married by the power of man within the parameters and the limits that are set; he has that prerogative by the agency that the Lord has given him. But if he wants a wife to be his in the realms ahead, he had better find someone who has power to bind on earth and seal in heaven.

In order to get a proper marriage one must do this: first, search for and seek out celestial marriage—find the right ordinance; second, look for a legal administrator, someone who holds the sealing power—and that power is exercised only in the temples that the Lord has had built by the tithing and sacrifice of his people in our day; and third, so live in righteousness, uprightness, integrity, virtue, and morality that he is entitled to have the Holy Spirit of God ratify and seal and justify and approve, and in that event his marriage is sealed by the Holy Spirit of promise and is binding in time and in eternity.

So we Latter-day Saints struggle and labor and work to be worthy to get a recommend to go to the temple, for the spirit will not dwell in an unclean tabernacle. We struggle and labor to get our tabernacles clean, to be pure and refined and cultured, to have the Spirit as our companion; and when we get in that state, our bishop and our stake president give us a "recommend" to go to the temple. We go there and make solemn and sober covenants, and having so done we then labor and struggle and work will all our power to continue in the light of the Spirit so that the agreement we have made will not be broken. If we do that, we have the assurance of eternal life. We do not need to tremble and fear; we do not need to have anxiety or worry if we are laboring and working and struggling to the best of our abilities. Though we do not become perfect, though we do not overcome all things, if our hearts are right and we are charting a course to eternal life in the manner I indicate, our marriages will continue in the realms that are ahead. We shall get into the paradise of God, and we shall be husband and wife. We shall come up in the resurrection, and we shall be husband and wife.

Anyone who comes up in the resurrection in the marriage state has the absolute guarantee of eternal life, but he will not then be a possessor and inheritor of all things—there is a great deal of progress and advancement to be made after the grave and after the resurrection. But he will be in the course where he will go on in the schooling and preparing processes until eventually he knows all things and becomes like God our Heavenly Father, meaning that he becomes an inheritor of eternal life.

In a manner of speaking we have, here and now, probationary families even though we have been married in the temple, because our marriage in the temple is conditional. It is conditioned upon our subsequent compliance with the laws, the terms, the conditions of the covenant that we then make. And so when I get married in the temple, I am put in a position where I can strive and labor and learn to love my wife with the perfection that must exist if I am going to have a fulness of the glory that attends this covenant in eternity, and it puts her in a position to learn to love me in the same way. It puts both of us in a position to bring up our children in light and truth and to school and prepare them to be members of an eternal family unit, and it puts us as children of our parents in a position where we honor our parents and do what is necessary to have these eternal ties go from one generation to the next and the next. Eventually there will be a great patriarchal chain of exalted beings from Adam to the last man, with any links left out being individuals who are not qualified and worthy to inherit, possess, and receive along the indicated line.

I am talking now to people who have opportunity to live the law. Anyone who has the opportunity is required to do so; it is mandatory. I am perfectly well aware that there are people who did not have the opportunity but who would have lived the law had the opportunity been afforded; and those individuals will be judged in the providence and mercy of a gracious God according to the intents and desires of their hearts. That is the principle of salvation and exaltation for the dead.

I have talked only in general terms; I have deliberately not been specific. I have designed to set forth true principles, as the Prophet indicated in his statement, "I teach them correct principles, and they govern themselves" (quoted by John Taylor, "The Organization of the Church," *Millennial Star,* November 1851, p. 3). I have desired and designed to set forth the general concept that is involved with the hope that, having the concept before us, each of us will then determine for ourselves the courses that we have to pursue as individuals to obtain the indicated rewards.

I think that the noblest concept that can enter the heart of man is the fact that the family unit continues in eternity. I do not think that one can conceive of a more glorious concept than that—building, of course, on the foundation of the atoning sacrifice of the Lord Jesus. Celestial marriage is the thing that opens the door to eternal life in our Father's kingdom. If we can pass the probationary experiences that prevail and exist in the family unit, then the Lord will say to us at some future day, "Well done, thou good and faithful servant: . . . enter thou into the joy of thy lord" (Matthew 25:21).

The things we are talking about here are true. That is the glory and the wonder and the beauty of everything connected with this system of revealed religion that we have—it is true. There is no more glorious fact connected with our whole system of revealed religion than the simple fact that it is true; and because it is true the doctrines that we teach are true; and because these doctrines are true, they will give us peace and joy and happiness in this life. They will enable us to cast off the drudgery, sludge, evil, and iniquities of the world; they will empower us to put on Christ and the glory and beauty of pure religion and to become new creatures of the Holy Ghost. It is a wondrous thing beyond belief to belong to a system that is true, that is founded on the rock foundation of eternal truth.

I hope, as I bear testimony to you of the truth and divinity of this work, that my words simply echo the thoughts that are in your hearts. I know just as well as I know anything in this world that God has spoken in our day, that Jesus is the Lord, that he has worked out the infinite and eternal atoning sacrifice, that the Lord has set up his kingdom for the last time among men, that Spencer W. Kimball at this moment is the prophet and revelator and mouthpiece of the Almighty on earth, and that this Church, weak and struggling and humble as it is now, is going to advance and grow and progress until the knowledge of God covers the earth as the waters cover the sea. Our destiny is to fill the earth because we are founded on the rock foundation of eternal truth. There is nothing in all this world like the gospel of the Lord Jesus Christ, and I bear witness of it and hope that, as you say amen, you will thus make my witness your witness and that you will then be under covenant to do the things that must be done to gain peace and joy in this life and to be an inheritor of eternal life in the world to come. In the name of the Lord Jesus Christ. Amen.

"All Are Alike unto God"

Bruce R. McConkie

I would like to say something about the new revelation relative to the priesthood going to those of all nations and races. "He [meaning Christ, who is the Lord God] inviteth them all to come unto him and partake of his goodness; and he denieth none that come unto him, black and white, bond and free, male and female; and he remembereth the heathen; and all are alike unto God, both Jew and Gentile" (2 Nephi 26:33).

These words have now taken on a new meaning. We have caught a new vision of their true significance. This also applies to a great number of other passages in the revelations. Since the Lord gave this revelation on the priesthood, our understanding of many passages has expanded. Many of us never imagined or supposed that they had the extensive and broad meaning that they do have.

I shall give you a few impressions relative to what has happened, and then attempt—if properly guided by the Spirit—to indicate to

This address was given at the CES Religious Educators Symposium on 18 August 1978.

you the great significance that this event has in the Church, in the world, and where the rolling forth of the great gospel is concerned.

The gospel goes to various peoples and nations on a priority basis. We were commanded in the early days of this dispensation to preach the gospel to every nation, kindred, tongue, and people. Our revelations talk about its going to every creature. There was, of course, no possible way for us to do all of this in the beginning days of our dispensation, nor can we now, in the full sense.

And so, guided by inspiration, we began to go from one nation and one culture to another. Someday, in the providences of the Lord, we shall get into Red China and Russia and the Middle East and so on, until eventually the gospel will have been preached everywhere, to all people; and this will occur before the Second Coming of the Son of Man.

Not only is the gospel to go, on a priority basis and harmonious to a divine timetable, to one nation after another, but the whole history of God's dealings with men on earth indicates that such has been the case in the past; it has been restricted and limited where many people are concerned. For instance, in the days between Moses and Christ, the gospel went to the house of Israel almost exclusively. By the time of Jesus, the legal administrators and prophetic associates that he had were so fully indoctrinated with the concept of having the gospel go only to the house of Israel that they were totally unable to envision the true significance of his proclamation that after the Resurrection they should then go to all the world. They did not go to the gentile nations initially. In his own ministration, Jesus preached only to the lost sheep of the house of Israel and had so commanded the Apostles (see Matthew 10:6).

It is true that he made few minor exceptions because of the faith and devotion of some Gentiles. There was one woman who wanted to eat the crumbs that fell from the table of the children, causing him to say, "O woman, great is thy faith" (Matthew 15:28; see also Mark 7:27–28). With some minor exceptions, the gospel in that day went exclusively to Israel. The Lord had to give Peter the vision and revelation of the sheet coming down from heaven with the unclean meat on it, following which Cornelius sent the messenger to Peter to learn what he, Cornelius, and his gentile associates should do. The Lord commanded them that the gospel go to the Gentiles, and so it was. There was about a quarter of a century, then, in New Testament times, when there were extreme difficulties among the Saints. They were weighing and evaluating, struggling with the problem of whether the gospel was to go only to the house of Israel or whether it now went to all men. Could all men come to him on an equal basis with the seed of Abraham?

There have been these problems, and the Lord has permitted them to arise. There isn't any question about that. We do not envision the whole reason and purpose behind all of it.

You know this principle: God "hath made of one blood all nations of men for to dwell on all the face of the earth, and hath determined the times before appointed, and the bounds of their habitation; That they should seek the Lord, if haply they might feel after him, and find him" (Acts 17:26–27)—meaning that there is an appointed time for successive nations and peoples and races and cultures to be offered the saving truths of the gospel. There are nations today to whom we have not gone—notably Red China and Russia. But you can rest assured that we will fulfill the requirement of taking the gospel to those nations before the Second Coming of the Son of Man.

And I have no hesitancy whatever in saying that before the Lord comes, in all those nations we will have congregations that are stable, secure, devoted, and sound. We will have stakes of Zion. We will have people who have progressed in spiritual things to the point where they have received all of the blessings of the house of the Lord. That is the destiny.

We have revelations that tell us that the gospel is to go to every nation, kindred, tongue, and people before the Second Coming of the Son of Man. And we have revelations which recite that when the Lord comes he will find those who speak every tongue and are members of every nation and kindred, who will be kings and priests, who will live and reign on earth with him a thousand years. That means,

as you know, that people from all nations will have the blessings of
the house of the Lord before the Second Coming.

We have read these passages and their associated passages for
many years. We have seen what the words say and have said to ourselves, "Yes, it says that, but we must read out of it the taking of the
gospel and the blessings of the temple to the Negro people, because
they are denied certain things." There are statements in our literature
by the early Brethren which we have interpreted to mean that the
Negroes would not receive the priesthood in mortality. I have said
the same things, and people write me letters and say, "You said such
and such, and how is it now that we do such and such?" And all I can
say to that is that it is time disbelieving people repented and got in
line and believed in a living, modern prophet. Forget everything that
I have said, or what President Brigham Young or President George
Q. Cannon or whomsoever has said in days past that is contrary to
the present revelation. We spoke with a limited understanding and
without the light and knowledge that now has come into the world.

We get our truth and our light line upon line and precept upon
precept. We have now had added a new flood of intelligence and light
on this particular subject, and it erases all the darkness and all the
views and all the thoughts of the past. They don't matter any more.

It doesn't make a particle of difference what anybody ever said
about the Negro matter before the first day of June of this year, 1978.
It is a new day and a new arrangement, and the Lord has now given
the revelation that sheds light out into the world on this subject.
As to any slivers of light or any particles of darkness of the past, we
forget about them. We now do what meridian Israel did when the
Lord said the gospel should go to the Gentiles. We forget all the
statements that limited the gospel to the house of Israel, and we start
going to the Gentiles.

Obviously, the Brethren have had a great anxiety and concern
about this problem for a long period of time, and President Spencer
W. Kimball has been exercised and has sought the Lord in faith.
When we seek the Lord on a matter, with sufficient faith and
devotion, he gives us an answer. You will recall that the Book of

Mormon teaches that if the Apostles in Jerusalem had asked the Lord, he would have told them about the Nephites. But they didn't ask, they didn't manifest that faith, and they didn't get an answer. One underlying reason for what happened to us is that the Brethren asked in faith; they petitioned and desired and wanted an answer—President Kimball in particular. And the other underlying principle is that in the eternal providences of the Lord, the time had come for extending the gospel to a race and a culture to whom it had previously been denied, at least as far as all of its blessings are concerned. So it was a matter of faith and righteousness and seeking on the one hand, and it was a matter of the divine timetable on the other hand. The time had arrived when the gospel, with all its blessings and obligations, should go to the Negro.

Well, in that setting, on the first day of June in this year, 1978, the First Presidency and the Twelve, after full discussion of the proposition and all the premises and principles that are involved, importuned the Lord for a revelation. President Kimball was mouth, and he prayed with great faith and great fervor; this was one of those occasions when an inspired prayer was offered. You know the Doctrine and Covenants statement that if we pray by the power of the Spirit we will receive answers to our prayers and it will be given us what we shall ask (see D&C 50:30). It was given President Kimball what he should ask. He prayed by the power of the Spirit, and there was perfect unity, total and complete harmony, between the Presidency and the Twelve on the issue involved.

And when President Kimball finished his prayer, the Lord gave a revelation by the power of the Holy Ghost. Revelation primarily comes by the power of the Holy Ghost. Always that member of the Godhead is involved. But most revelations, from the beginning to now, have come in that way. There have been revelations given in various ways on other occasions. The Father and the Son appeared in the Sacred Grove. Moroni, an angel from heaven, came relative to instructing the Prophet in the affairs that were destined to occur in this dispensation. There have been visions, notably the vision of the degrees of glory. There may be an infinite number of ways that God

can ordain that revelations come. But, primarily, revelation comes
by the power of the Holy Ghost. The principle is set forth in the
Doctrine and Covenants, section 68, that whatever the elders of the
Church speak, when moved upon by the power of the Holy Ghost,
shall be scripture, shall be the mind and will and voice of the Lord
(see verse 4).

On this occasion, because of the importuning and the faith, and
because the hour and the time had arrived, the Lord in his providences poured out the Holy Ghost upon the First Presidency and
the Twelve in a miraculous and marvelous manner, beyond anything
that any then present had ever experienced. The revelation came to
the president of the Church; it also came to each individual present.
There were ten members of the Council of the Twelve and three of
the First Presidency there assembled. The result was that President
Kimball knew, and each one of us knew, independent of any other
person, by direct and personal revelation to us, that the time had now
come to extend the gospel and all its blessings and all its obligations,
including the priesthood and the blessings of the house of the Lord,
to those of every nation, culture, and race, including the black race.
There was no question whatsoever as to what happened or as to the
word and message that came.

The revelation came to the president of the Church and, in
harmony with Church government, was announced by him; the
announcement was made eight days later over the signature of the
First Presidency. But in this instance, in addition to the revelation
coming to the man who would announce it to the Church and to the
world and who was sustained as the mouthpiece of God on earth,
the revelation came to every member of the body that I have named.
They all knew it in the temple.

In my judgment this was done by the Lord in this way because
it was a revelation of such tremendous significance and import; one
which would reverse the whole direction of the Church, procedur-
ally and administratively; one which would affect the living and the
dead; one which would affect the total relationship that we have
with the world; one, I say, of such significance that the Lord wanted

independent witnesses who could bear record that the thing had happened.

Now if President Kimball had received the revelation and had asked for a sustaining vote, obviously he would have received it and the revelation would have been announced. But the Lord chose this other course, in my judgment, because of the tremendous import and the eternal significance of what was being revealed. This affects our missionary work and all of our preaching to the world. This affects our genealogical research and all of our temple ordinances. This affects what is going on in the spirit world, because the gospel is preached in the spirit world preparatory to men's receiving the vicarious ordinances which make them heirs to salvation and exaltation. This is a revelation of tremendous significance.

The vision of the degrees of glory begins by saying, "Hear, O ye heavens, and give ear, O earth" (D&C 76:1). In other words, in that revelation the Lord was announcing truth to heaven and to earth because those principles of salvation operate on both sides of the veil; and salvation is administered to an extent here to men, and it is administered to another extent in the spirit world. We correlate and combine our activities and do certain things for the salvation of men while we are in mortality, and then certain things are done for the salvation of men while they are in the spirit world awaiting the day of the Resurrection.

Well, once again a revelation was given that affects this sphere of activity and the sphere that is to come. And so it had tremendous significance; the eternal import was such that it came in the way it did. The Lord could have sent messengers from the other side to deliver it, but he did not. He gave the revelation by the power of the Holy Ghost. Latter-day Saints have a complex: many of them desire to magnify and build upon what has occurred, and they delight to think of miraculous things. And maybe some of them would like to believe that the Lord himself was there, or that the Prophet Joseph Smith came to deliver the revelation (see *Time*, 7 August 1978, p. 55), which was one of the possibilities. Well, these things did not happen. The stories that go around to the contrary are not factual or realistic or true, and you as teachers in the Church Educational System will be in a position to explain and to tell your students that this thing came by the power of the Holy Ghost and that all the Brethren involved, the thirteen who were present, are independent personal witnesses of the truth and divinity of what occurred.

There is no way to describe in language what is involved. This cannot be done. You are familiar with Book of Mormon references where the account says that no tongue could tell and no pen could write what was involved in the experience and that it had to be felt by the power of the Spirit. This was one of those occasions. To carnal people who do not understand the operating of the Holy Spirit of God upon the souls of man, this may sound like gibberish or jargon or uncertainty or ambiguity; but to those who are enlightened by the power of the Spirit and who have themselves felt its power, it will have a ring of veracity and truth, and they will know of its verity. I cannot describe in words what happened; I can only say that it happened and that it can be known and understood only by the feeling that can come into the heart of man. You cannot describe a testimony to someone. No one can really know what a testimony is—the feeling and the joy and the rejoicing and the happiness that comes into the heart of man when he gets one—except another person who has received a testimony. Some things can be known only by revelation, "The things of God knoweth no man, but the Spirit of God" (1 Corinthians 2:11).

This is a brief explanation of what was involved in this new revelation. I think I can add that it is one of the signs of the times. It is something that had to occur before the Second Coming. It was something that was mandatory and imperative in order to enable us to fulfill all of the revelations that are involved, in order to spread the gospel in the way that the scriptures say it must spread before the Lord comes, in order for all of the blessings to come to all of the people, according to the promises. It is one of the signs of the times. This revelation which came on the first day of June was reaffirmed by the spirit of inspiration one week later on June 8, when the Brethren approved the document that was to be announced to the world. And then it was reaffirmed the next day, on Friday, June 9, with all of the General Authorities present in the temple, that is, all who were available. All received the assurance and witness and confirmation by the power of the Spirit that what had occurred was the mind, the will, the intent, and the purpose of the Lord.

Well, this is a glorious day. This is a wondrous thing; the veil is thin. The Lord is not far distant from his church. He is not far removed.

President Kimball is a man of almost infinite spiritual capacity— a tremendous spiritual giant. The Lord has magnified him beyond any understanding or expression and has given him His mind and His will on a great number of vital matters which have altered the course of the past—one of which is the organization of the First Quorum of the Seventy. As you know, the Church is being guided and led by the power of the Holy Ghost, and the Lord's hand is in it. There is no question whatever about that. And we are doing the right thing where this matter is concerned.

There has been a tremendous feeling of gratitude and thanks-giving in the hearts of members of the Church everywhere, with isolated exceptions. There are individuals who are out of harmony on this and on plural marriage and on other doctrines, but for all general purposes there has been universal acceptance; and everyone who has been in tune with the Spirit has known that the Lord spoke and that his mind and his purposes are being manifest to the course the Church is pursuing. We have already called our first Negro elder. He has been assigned to serve in the Florida Fort Lauderdale Mission. We have already called our first Negro sister, assigned to the Brazil Rio de Janeiro Mission. This race and culture now is going to be one with us in bearing the burdens of the kingdom.

We talk about the scriptures being unfolded—read over again the parable of the laborers in the vineyard (see Matthew 20) and remind yourselves that those who labor through the heat of the day for twelve hours are going to be rewarded the same as those who came in at the third and the sixth and the eleventh hours. Well, it is the eleventh hour; it is the Saturday night of time. In this eleventh hour the Lord has given the blessings of the gospel to the last group of laborers in the vineyard. And when he metes out his rewards, when he makes his payments, according to the accounts and the scriptural statements, he will give the penny to all, whether it is for one hour or twelve hours of work. All are alike unto God, black and white, bond and free, male and female.

Joseph Smith: A Revealer of Christ

Bruce R. McConkie

I devoutly and sincerely hope that we may have a rich outpouring of the Holy Spirit, for two reasons: first, so that I may say what the Lord wants said and what he would say if he personally were here; and secondly, so that those words will sink into your hearts and you will know of a surety that they are true. I shall take as a subject, "Joseph Smith: A Revealer of Christ."

I have chosen a text statement. These words were prepared and published by the First Presidency of the Church in 1935 on the occasion of the one hundredth anniversary of the organization of the first Quorum of Twelve Apostles in our dispensation:

Two great truths must be accepted by mankind if they shall save themselves: first, that Jesus is the Christ, the Messiah, the Only Begotten, the very Son of God, whose atoning blood and resurrection save us from the physical and spiritual death brought to us by the fall; and next, that God has restored to the earth, in these last days, through the Prophet Joseph Smith, His holy Priesthood with the fulness of the everlasting Gospel, for

This fireside address was given at Brigham Young University on 3 September 1978.

the salvation of all men on the earth. Without these truths man may not hope for the riches of the life hereafter. [*The Improvement Era*, April 1935, pp. 204–5]

We have a great pattern, a revealed pattern interwoven in all of the revelations that have been given in all ages, that indicates how salvation is made available to men on earth. As we are all aware, we are here on earth as the spirit children of God, our Heavenly Father. We are here inhabiting bodies—tabernacles made of clay—to be tried and examined and tested to see if we will do all things that the Lord directs and commands for his children generally and for each of us in particular. We are here to see if we will believe eternal truth and if we will conform to the principles so accepted and so learned. And if we believe and obey, we manage to do the things that will enable us, first, to have peace and joy and happiness in this life, and secondly, to go on to eternal reward in our Father's kingdom.

For every age in which the gospel is given, for every gospel dispensation, for every time that a gracious God dispenses the plan of salvation to his children on earth, he follows an identical pattern: he reveals two great truths which apply to the dispensation involved. One of these truths applies to all dispensations and the other to the specific dispensation. The truth of universal application for all men in all ages from father Adam to the last man is that salvation is in Christ; that he is the Redeemer and Savior of men; that in and through his atoning sacrifice, by the blood that he shed and the redemption that he wrought, salvation is available for all men. Because of Christ, all men will be raised in immortality, and those who believe and obey will then be raised unto eternal life in our Father's kingdom.

Immortality, by definition and in its nature, is to live everlastingly with a body of flesh and bones; it is to be resurrected; it is to have body and spirit inseparably connected. Eternal life, on the other hand, is, for one thing, to live eternally in the family unit and, for another thing, to inherit, possess, and receive the dignity, honor, power, and glory of God himself. Anyone for whom the family unit continues in eternity will have eternal life, and in process of time he will acquire all the dignity, honor, glory, power, might, and omnipotence that the Eternal Father possesses.

Immortality comes because of the Lord Jesus Christ; it is a free gift for all men. Eternal life is made available through the same atoning sacrifice, and it is a gift to all who obey the law upon which its receipt is predicated. The laws of salvation are the same for every age. They have never varied, and they will never vary. Every man from Adam to the last soul to inhabit this earth must do precisely and exactly the same things and obey the same laws in order to inherit, receive, and possess the same glory in eternity.

Salvation is in Christ, and in order for men to believe and obey, the laws of Christ and the doctrine of Christ—which comprise his everlasting gospel—must be revealed in whatever age is involved. That is a universal, unvarying requirement. The gospel did not originate in the meridian of time—it did not start when the Lord Jesus was upon earth. It is an everlasting gospel. It commenced in the beginning, it has come down in successive periods or dispensations from the days of Adam to the present, and it will continue as long as men are on earth. Always and everlastingly, salvation will be in Christ.

But we need a revealer of the knowledge of salvation for whatever dispensation is involved. Our revelation says, "Salvation was, and is, and is to come, in and through the atoning blood of Christ, the Lord Omnipotent" (Mosiah 3:18). We need make no mistake about that. Our affection, our interest, our concern, our love, our devotion—all that we have and all that we possess is centered in the Lord Jesus; but, having said that affirmatively and unequivocally and positively, we come to the fact that a revealer of the knowledge of Christ and of salvation is needed for every age of the earth. Thus we find such a thing in our revelations as this: "Joseph Smith, the Prophet and Seer of the Lord, has done more, save Jesus only, for the salvation of men in this world, than any other man that ever lived in it" (D&C 135:3). And so, for our dispensation, we link the names of Christ and of Joseph Smith.

Now I read you these words of Brigham Young:

*Who can justly say aught against Joseph Smith? I was as well
acquainted with him, as any man. I do not believe that his father and
mother knew him any better than I did. I do not think that a man lives on
the earth that knew him any better than I did; and I am bold to say that,
Jesus Christ excepted, no better man ever lived or does live upon this earth.
I am his witness. He was persecuted for the same reason that any other righteous person has been or is persecuted at the present day.* [John A. Widtsoe,
comp., *Discourses of Brigham Young*, 2d ed., pp. 702–3]

Let us gain a true vision; let us reason together and figure out
how the Lord operates with reference to his children. First of all, we
read in the visions of Abraham about the noble and great in the premortal life who were foreordained. Abraham is told that he is one of
them. They are identified as the offspring of the Father, as spirits, as
souls; and then the account says, "And there stood one among them
that was like unto God" (Abraham 3:24). This is the Lord Jesus, the
Lord Jehovah. This is the firstborn in the spirit, who, through righteousness and zealousness and obedience, became "like unto God,"
meaning unto the Father.

And he [that is, Christ] *said unto those who were with him* [the host
of noble and great ones, the ones Abraham had seen]: *We will go down*
[not I, Jehovah, alone, but we, the noble and great, the mighty and
valiant sons of our Father; we will go down], *for there is space there,
and we will take of these materials, and we will make an earth whereon
these* [that is, the spirit hosts of heaven] *may dwell;*
*And we will prove them herewith, to see if they will do all things
whatsoever the Lord their God shall command them.* [Abraham 3:24–25]

Who is listed and counted in that great council of eternity, that
assemblage of the noble and great seen by Abraham? There is not
much question in our minds; they were the people who were foreordained to minister to men in this world.

We know a little bit about the order of priority, the precedence,
and the rank that is involved. We know that the Lord Jesus was

number one: mighty, superior, valiant, intelligent above all others. We know that a spirit named Michael was number two, and that he was born into this world as Adam, the first man. We know that a spirit named Gabriel stood third in preeminence, might, and power, and that he came among us as Noah.

After that we cannot specifically and definitely categorize the various spirits; but we do know that the noblest and the greatest and the mightiest among them were ordained to be heads of dispensations—to be the individuals who, for their era and age and dispensation, would commence the spread of eternal truth on earth. We know, for instance, with reference to Moses, who was the head of one of these dispensations, that "there arose not a prophet . . . in Israel like unto Moses, whom the Lord knew face to face" (Deuteronomy 34:10). That sets us a pattern. We know of men like Enoch, who so lived that he perfected his whole city and his whole people, and they were translated and taken up into heaven. We look back at Abraham and consider him to be the Father of the Faithful and rejoice that we are born as his seed.

There is a limited number of mighty, noble spirits who headed the respective dispensations. How many we do not know; perhaps there were eight or ten or twenty, but the number does not matter. At any rate, we soon have a small group of select individuals who stand in intelligence and power and might next to the Lord Jehovah. In the same sense that he was like unto God, these chosen and select individuals who were destined to head his work for these long ages were like unto Christ.

When sifting out the relative importance of individuals, without knowing the details, we can conclude that a man born in modern times to head this dispensation was like unto Adam, like unto Moses, like unto Abraham, like unto Christ—in other words, was one of the ten or twenty noblest and greatest spirits who, up to this time, have been born into mortality. He and hosts with him performed their labors and their work in the creative enterprises that brought this earth rolling into existence, and he and his associates headed the periods of time when eternal truth went out to the sons of men.

That is how we rank and place the prophet Joseph Smith: he is one of the great dispensation heads, and a dispensation head is a revealer for his age and his period of the knowledge of Christ and of salvation. Thus, the other prophets of the dispensation who are associated with him and who come after him, who sustain his work and bear record of him, become witnesses that he—the chief prophet of their age—revealed the Lord Jesus and hence made salvation available.

This means that in a testimony meeting in our day we link the name of Joseph Smith with that of Jesus Christ. We stand up and say, "I know that Jesus Christ is the Son of the living God and that he was crucified for the sins of the world." And in the next breath we say, "I know that Joseph Smith, Junior, was chosen, appointed, anointed, and called as God's prophet for this age in order to reveal Christ and to reveal salvation." We bear witness of Christ, and we bear witness of Joseph Smith.

That is the way it has been from the beginning. There have always been testimony meetings. If we had lived in the days of Adam and had assembled to worship the Lord, the Spirit would have rested mightily upon us on occasions, and we would have said, "I know that salvation is in Christ who shall come, and I know that Adam, our father, is a legal administrator who holds keys and powers and authority and that he is the revealer of the knowledge of Christ and of salvation for men on earth."

If we had lived in the days of Enoch, we would have arisen in our testimony meetings and said, "I testify of Christ, and I testify of Enoch, who revealed Christ, and automatically I believe also in Adam who went before." That pattern would also have been followed in Noah's day, in Abraham's day, in Melchizedek's day, and in every age when eternal truth has been revealed. Always we would have linked the name of Christ and the name of the dispensation head, and automatically we would have believed in every prophet that went before.

We cannot suppose for one minute that it would be possible for someone who lived in the days of the Lord Jesus to believe that he was the son of God and yet to reject the witness of Peter, James, and

John. That is a philosophical impossibility. Had we lived in that day it would not have been possible to say, "Well, I'll believe in Christ; but I won't believe in Peter, James, and John, his apostles, who have revealed him to me and who have borne witness of his divine Sonship." The Lord and his prophets always go together. With that in mind let me read these words of Brigham Young:

Whosoever confesseth that Joseph Smith was sent of God to reveal the holy Gospel to the children of men, and lay the foundation for gathering Israel, and building up the kingdom of God on the earth, that spirit is of God; and every spirit that does not confess that God has sent Joseph Smith, and revealed the everlasting Gospel to and through him, is of Antichrist, no matter whether it is found in a pulpit or on a throne. [JD 8:176–77]

Having these concepts and these expressions in mind, I am going to read to you some passages given and spoken by the Lord Jesus, in which he associates himself with John the Baptist. Out of these passages we shall have an affirmation and a reaffirmation of the truth and concept that Christ and his prophets go together, that it is not possible to believe in one without believing in the other, and that by rejecting the prophets we reject Christ himself. Jesus said this:

If I bear witness of myself, yet my witness is true.

For I am not alone, there is another who beareth witness of me, and I know that the testimony which he giveth of me is true.

Ye sent unto John, and he bare witness also unto the truth.

And he received not his testimony of man, but of God, and ye yourselves say that he is a prophet, therefore ye ought to receive his testimony. [John 5:32–35; Joseph Smith Translation of the Bible, hereafter cited as JST; all biblical references without this notation come from the King James Version]

John bore as persuasive and powerful a testimony as we know of or find in any written record. On those occasions of Christ's visits to him near Bethabara, as he baptized in Jordan, he said, "Behold

the Lamb of God, which taketh away the sin of the world" (John
1:29). That was simply a text statement or a subject head for long
discourses that he obviously preached about the divine Sonship. On
one occasion John said this—and it is as blunt and as plain as any
witness—"He that believeth on the Son hath everlasting life: and he
that believeth not the Son shall not see life; but the wrath of God
abideth on him" (John 3:36). John said, in effect, "Here is Jesus; he is
the Son of God." There was no possible way to believe that John was
a prophet and reject the Lord Jesus. To accept one was to accept the
other. Jesus said,

*John came unto you in the way of righteousness, and bore record of me, and
ye believed him not; but the publicans and the harlots believed him; and ye,
afterward, when ye had seen me, repented not, that ye might believe him.*

*For he that believed not John concerning me, cannot believe me, except
he first repent.*

*And except ye repent, the preaching of John shall condemn you in the
day of judgment.* [Matthew 21:32–34; JST]

We could recite that over again, paraphrasing the language, and apply
it to Joseph Smith and his situation in our day.

Here is another passage:

*Then said the Pharisees unto him, Why will ye not receive us with our
baptism, seeing we keep the whole law?*

*But Jesus said unto them, Ye keep not the law. If ye had kept the law,
ye would have received me, for I am he who gave the law.*

I receive not you with your baptism, because it profiteth you nothing.

For when that which is new is come, the old is ready to be put away.
[Matthew 9:18–21; JST]

Following those expressions came the ones with which we are so
familiar, about putting new wine in old bottles. In other words, we
have new revelation in our day in a new church, just as the case was
in the meridian dispensation.

Then certain of them came to him, saying, Good Master, we have Moses and the prophets, and whosoever shall live by them, shall he not have life?

And Jesus answered, saying, Ye know not Moses, neither the prophets; for if ye had known them, ye would have believed on me; for to this intent they were written. For I am sent that ye might have life. [Luke 14:35–36; JST]

The principle that the Lord and his prophets go together is a glorious one. Here are some words I wrote on this subject on one occasion.

Living Oracles
We be Abraham's children, the Jews said to Jove;
We shall follow our Father, inherit his trove.
But from Jesus our Lord, came the stinging rebuke:
Ye are children of him, whom ye list to obey;
Were ye Abraham's seed, ye would walk in his path,
And escape the strong chains of the father of wrath.

We have Moses the seer, and the prophets of old;
All their words we shall treasure as silver and gold.
But from Jesus our Lord, came the sobering voice;
If to Moses ye turn, then give heed to his word;
Only then can ye hope for rewards of great worth,
For he spake of my coming and labors on earth.

We have Peter and Paul, in their steps let us trod;
So religionists say, as they worship their God.
But speaks He who is Lord of the living and dead:
In the hands of those prophets, those teachers and seers,
Who abide in your day have I given the keys;
Unto them ye must turn, the Eternal to please.

With those principles in mind, let us be vividly and acutely aware of their application to Joseph Smith. One of our revelations says— in the words of the Lord Jesus, speaking to Joseph Smith—"This generation shall have my word through you" (D&C 5:10). I think He made that statement, either in those verbatim words or in thought content, to every dispensation head there has been. I think he said it to Enoch, Moses, Abraham, and in principle to all: "This genera-tion shall have my word through you." Someone has to reveal eternal truth, and these brethren whom I have mentioned are the ones to whom the Lord gave that obligation.

Therefore, we find such directives as this, spoken by the Lord to the Church immediately following its organization on the sixth day of April in 1830. He is talking about Joseph Smith:

Thou [the Church] *shalt give heed unto all his words and commandments which he shall give unto you as he receiveth them, walking in all holiness before me;*

[Now note:] *For his word ye shall receive, as if from mine own mouth, in all patience and faith. . . .* [This sets a dispensation head apart from all other prophets. Here is the subsequent statement about him:]

. . . Behold, I will bless all those who labor in my vineyard with a mighty blessing, and they shall believe on his words, which are given him through me by the Comforter, which manifesteth that Jesus was crucified by sinful men for the sins of the world, yea, for the remission of sins unto the contrite heart. [D&C 21:4–5, 9]

What is the measure of our discipleship? How do we measure and test how firmly we are rooted in the restored faith? I think one of the great tests is the degree and the extent, the fervor and sincer-ity, the devotion and true belief that we give to the words that came from the Prophet Joseph Smith. Here is a man that, first of all, gave us the Book of Mormon—the Book of Mormon, which is an account of God's dealings with a people who had the fullness of the gospel, which bears record of Christ, which recounts in plainness and in simplicity the basic and fundamental truths that men must believe to be saved. Here is a man who gave a book of incomparable value—his words, as it were to us, at least, because it was through his instru-mentality that they came. Here is a man who gave us the revelations in the Doctrine and Covenants—revelations which speak in the first person, with the Lord Jesus himself being mouth and voice but the lips being the lips of Joseph Smith—a volume of revealed truth where God Almighty speaks through his prophet.

Here are words that the Prophet gave us in the Pearl of Great Price, the Book of Moses being taken from Joseph Smith's translation of the scriptures and the Book of Abraham being translated from the papyrus. Here are words in many places in the Joseph Smith Translation itself, revealed words that come from God by prophetic power. Here are sermons—majestic, wondrous, marvelous sermons which recount the mind and will and plan and purposes of the Lord to men on earth—for instance, the King Follet sermon from which President Kimball quoted copiously at the funeral sermon of Brother Stapley recently.

We speak about judging a man by his fruits, and among the great fruits of Joseph Smith are the words that he spoke, the words that he wrote, the inspired message that he gave. I suggest that a measure of discipleship, a standard of judgment whereby we can tell how firmly we are anchored in the faith of the Lord, is how sincerely and completely we believe the words that have come from the Prophet Joseph Smith. Obviously incident to this, we have an obligation and a need to treasure up these words, to search out these truths, to learn what they are, and then to make them a living part of us.

We bear testimony of Christ, and we do it with all the fervor and conviction and power of our whole soul, striving and laboring to do it by the power of the Holy Ghost; and as our voices echo and reecho the eternal verity that Christ is the Lord, we say also that Joseph Smith is a prophet of God, a legal administrator who had power from God—keys and authority—so that he could bind on earth and have it sealed eternally in the heavens. Here, we say, is Joseph Smith, a revealer of the knowledge of Christ and of salvation for our day. We link the words together in one great testimony of eternal truth; and the reason we have power to bear witness of Christ, through whom salvation comes, is that Joseph Smith, the prophet and seer of the Lord for our day and in our day, has received eternal truth, has borne witness, has given revelation, has laid the foundation.

Brigham Young once said, "I feel like shouting Hallelujah, all the time, when I think that I ever knew Joseph Smith" (*Discourses of Brigham Young*, p. 458); and that is as it ought to be, because salvation is in Christ and salvation is available because Joseph Smith revealed Christ to the world. The world either accepts that witness and believes in the Lord's prophets or goes its way and at its peril loses the hope of eternal salvation. One must believe in Adam and Christ, if living in that day; or in Abraham and Christ, if living in that day; or in Moses and Christ, if living then; or, in our day, in Joseph Smith and Jesus Christ, crying "Hosanna" and "Hallelujah" and "Praise the Lord" whenever their names are mentioned by the power of the Holy Spirit.

I am grateful beyond any measure of expression I have that in my soul there rests the absolute, certain conviction that Jesus is the Lord. I know that as well as I know anything in this world. In that same sense—with unshaken certainty and absolute, pure, revealed knowledge—I know that Joseph Smith, Junior, who headed this dispensation, was the Lord's prophet for our day and our time; and that, as he certified, he saw in the spring of 1820 the Father and the Son; and that, as he certified, the revelations and the truths that fell from his lips are the voice and mind and will and purposes of the Lord for me and for all men in our day.

I pray God our Father that we may be valiant and true, that we may stand affirmatively and courageously in bearing witness of Christ—because salvation is in Christ and in none other—and that we will have the same fervor and the same devotion in linking the mighty and noble name of the head of our dispensation with the name of the Savior himself.

This I do by way of doctrine and by way of testimony on this occasion in the name of the Lord Jesus Christ. Amen.

The Seven Deadly Heresies

———◆———

Bruce R. McConkie

I have sought and do now seek that guidance and enlightenment which comes from the Holy Spirit of God. I desire to speak by the power of the Holy Ghost so that my words will be true and wise and proper. When any of us speak by the power of the Spirit, we say what the Lord wants said, or, better, what he would say if he were here in person.

I shall depart from my normal and usual pattern and read portions of my presentation because I want to state temperately and accurately the doctrinal principles involved and to say them in a way that will not leave room for doubt or question. I shall speak on some matters that some may consider to be controversial, though they ought not to be. They are things on which we ought to be united, and to the extent we are all guided and enlightened from on high we will be. If we are so united—and there will be no disagreement among those who believe and understand the revealed word—we will progress and advance and grow in the things of the Spirit; we will prepare

This fireside address was given at Brigham Young University on 1 June 1980.

ourselves for a life of peace and happiness and joy here and now, and
for an eventual eternal reward in the kingdom of our Father.

There is a song or a saying or a proverb or a legend or a tradition
or something that speaks of seven deadly sins. I know nothing
whatever about these and hope you do not. My subject is one about
which some few of you, unfortunately, do know a little. It is "The
Seven Deadly Heresies"—not the great heresies of a lost and fallen
Christendom, but some that have crept in among us.

Now I take a text. These words were written by Paul to certain
ancient Saints. In principle they apply to us:

> *I hear that there be divisions among you; and I partly believe it.*
>
> *For there must be also heresies among you, that they which are approved
> may be made manifest among you.* [1 Corinthians 11:18–19]

Now let me list some axioms (I guess in academic circles we call
these caveats):

—There is no salvation in believing a false doctrine.

—Truth, diamond truth, truth unmixed with error, truth alone
leads to salvation.

—What we believe determines what we do.

—No man can be saved in ignorance of God and his laws.

—Man is saved no faster than he gains knowledge of Jesus Christ
and the saving truths of his everlasting gospel.

—Gospel doctrines belong to the Lord, not to men. They are
his. He ordained them, he reveals them, and he expects us to believe
them.

—The doctrines of salvation are not discovered in a laboratory
or on a geological field trip or by accompanying Darwin around the
world. They come by revelation and in no other way.

—Our sole concern in seeking truth should be to learn and
believe what the Lord knows and believes. Providentially he has set
forth some of his views in the holy scriptures.

—Our goal as mortals is to gain the mind of Christ, to believe what he believes, to think what he thinks, to say what he says, to do what he does, and to be as he is.

—We are called upon to reject all heresies and cleave unto all truth. Only then can we progress according to the divine plan. As the Lord has said,

Whatever principle of intelligence we attain unto in this life, it will rise with us in the resurrection.

And if a person gains more knowledge and intelligence in this life through his diligence and obedience than another, he will have so much the advantage in the world to come. [D&C 130:18–19]

Please note that knowledge is gained by obedience. It comes by obedience to the laws and ordinances of the gospel. In the ultimate and full sense it comes only by revelation from the Holy Ghost. There are some things a sinful man does not and cannot know. The Lord's people are promised: "By the power of the Holy Ghost ye may know the truth of all things" (Moroni 10:5). But if they do not seek the Spirit, if they do not accept the revelations God has given, if they cannot distinguish between the revealed word and the theories of men, they have no promise of gaining a fullness of truth by the power of the Holy Ghost.

Now may I suggest the list of heresies.

Heresy one: There are those who say that God is progressing in knowledge and is learning new truths.

This is false—utterly, totally, and completely. There is not one sliver of truth in it. It grows out of a wholly twisted and incorrect view of the King Follett Sermon and of what is meant by eternal progression.

God progresses in the sense that his kingdoms increase and his dominions multiply—not in the sense that he learns new truths and discovers new laws. God is not a student. He is not a laboratory technician. He is not postulating new theories on the basis of past experiences. He has indeed graduated to that state of exaltation that consists of knowing all things and having all power.

The life that God lives is named *eternal life*. His name, one of them, is Eternal, using that word as a noun and not as an adjective, and he uses that name to identify the type of life that he lives. God's life is eternal life, and eternal life is God's life. They are one and the same. Eternal life is the reward we shall obtain if we believe and obey and walk uprightly before him. And eternal life consists of two things. It consists of life in the family unit, and, also, of inheriting, receiving, and possessing the fullness of the glory of the Father. Anyone who has each of these things is an inheritor and possessor of the greatest of all gifts of God, which is eternal life.

Eternal progression consists of living the kind of life God lives and of increasing in kingdoms and dominions everlastingly. Why anyone should suppose that an infinite and eternal being who has presided in our universe for almost 2,555,000,000 years, who made the sidereal heavens, whose creations are more numerous than the particles of the earth, and who is aware of the fall of every sparrow— why anyone would suppose that such a being has more to learn and new truths to discover in the laboratories of eternity is totally beyond my comprehension.

Will he one day learn something that will destroy the plan of salvation and turn man and the universe into an uncreated nothing- ness? Will he discover a better plan of salvation than the one he has already given to men in worlds without number?

The saving truth, as revealed to and taught, formally and officially, by the Prophet Joseph Smith in the *Lectures on Faith* is that God is omnipotent, omniscient, and omnipresent. He knows all things, he has all power, and he is everywhere present by the power of his Spirit. And unless we know and believe this doctrine we cannot gain faith unto life and salvation.

Joseph Smith also taught in the *Lectures on Faith* "that three things are necessary in order that any rational and intelligent being may exercise faith in God unto life and salvation." These he named as—

1. The idea that he actually exists;

2. A *correct* idea of his character, perfections, and attributes; and

3. An actual knowledge that the course of life which he is pursuing is according to the divine will.

The attributes of God are given as knowledge, faith or power, justice, judgment, mercy, and truth. The perfections of God are named as "the perfections which belong to all of the attributes of his nature," which is to say that God possesses and has all knowledge, all faith or power, all justice, all judgment, all mercy, and all truth. He is indeed the very embodiment and personification and source of all these attributes. Does anyone suppose that God can be more honest than he already is? Neither need any suppose there are truths he does not know or knowledge he does not possess.

Thus Joseph Smith taught, and these are his words:

> *Without the knowledge of all things, God would not be able to save any portion of his creatures; for it is by reason of the knowledge which he has of all things, from the beginning to the end, that enables him to give that understanding to his creatures by which they are made partakers of eternal life; and if it were not for the idea existing in the minds of men that God had all knowledge it would be impossible for them to exercise faith in him.* [As quoted by Bruce R. McConkie in *Mormon Doctrine* (Salt Lake City: Bookcraft, 1966), p. 264]

If God is just dabbling with a few truths he has already chanced to learn or experimenting with a few facts he has already discovered, we have no idea as to the real end and purpose of creation.

Heresy two concerns itself with the relationship between organic evolution and revealed religion and asks the question whether they can be harmonized.

There are those who believe that the theory of organic evolution runs counter to the plain and explicit principles set forth in the holy scriptures as these have been interpreted and taught by Joseph Smith and his associates. There are others who think that evolution is the system used by the Lord to form plant and animal life and to place man on earth.

May I say that all truth is in agreement, that true religion and true science bear the same witness, and that in the true and full sense, true science is part of true religion. But may I also raise some questions of a serious nature. Is there any way to harmonize the false religions of the Dark Ages with the truths of science as they have now been discovered? Is there any way to harmonize the revealed religion that has come to us with the theoretical postulates of Darwinism and the diverse speculations descending therefrom?

Should we accept the famous document of the First Presidency issued in the days of President Joseph F. Smith and entitled "The Origin of Man" as meaning exactly what it says? Is it the doctrine of the gospel that Adam stood next to Christ in power and might and intelligence before the foundations of the world were laid; that Adam was placed on this earth as an immortal being; that there was no death in the world for him or for any form of life until after the Fall; that the fall of Adam brought temporal and spiritual death into the world; that this temporal death passed upon all forms of life, upon man and animal and fish and fowl and plant life; that Christ came to ransom man and all forms of life from the effects of the temporal death brought into the world through the Fall, and in the case of man from a spiritual death also; and that this ransom includes a resurrection for man and for all forms of life? Can you harmonize these things with the evolutionary postulate that death has always existed and that the various forms of life have evolved from preceding forms over astronomically long periods of time?

Can you harmonize the theories of men with the inspired words that say:

And now, behold, if Adam had not transgressed he would not have fallen, but he would have remained in the garden of Eden. And all things which were created must have remained in the same state in which they were after they were created; and they must have remained forever, and had no end.

And they [meaning Adam and Eve] *would have had no children; wherefore they would have remained in a state of innocence, having no joy, for they knew no misery; doing no good, for they knew no sin.*

But behold, all things have been done in the wisdom of him who knoweth all things.

Adam fell that men might be; and men are, that they might have joy.

And the Messiah cometh in the fulness of time, that he may redeem the children of men from the fall. [2 Nephi 2:22–26]

These are questions to which all of us should find answers. Every person must choose for himself what he will believe. I recommend that all of you study and ponder and pray and seek light and knowledge in these and in all fields.

I believe that the atonement of Christ is the great and eternal foundation upon which revealed religion rests. I believe that no man can be saved unless he believes that our Lord's atoning sacrifice brings immortality to all and eternal life to those who believe and obey, and no man can believe in the atonement unless he accepts both the divine sonship of Christ and the fall of Adam.

My reasoning causes me to conclude that if death has always prevailed in the world, then there was no fall of Adam that brought death to all forms of life; that if Adam did not fall, there is no need for an atonement; that if there was no atonement, there is no salvation, no resurrection, and no eternal life; and that if there was no atonement, there is nothing in all of the glorious promises that the Lord has given us. I believe that the Fall affects man, all forms of life, and the earth itself, and that the Atonement affects man, all forms of life, and the earth itself.

Heresy three: There are those who say that temple marriage assures us of an eventual exaltation. Some have supposed that couples married in the temple who commit all manner of sin, and who then pay the penalty, will gain their exaltation eventually.

This notion is contrary to the whole system and plan that the Lord has ordained, a system under which we are privileged to work out our salvation with fear and trembling before him. If we believe and obey, if we enter the waters of baptism and make solemn covenants with the Lord to keep his commandments, we thereby get on a strait and narrow path that leads from the gate of repentance and baptism to a reward that is called eternal life. And if we traverse the length of the path going upward and forward and onward, keeping the commandments, loving the Lord, and doing all that we ought to do, eventually we will be inheritors of that reward.

And in exactly and precisely the same sense, celestial marriage is a gate that puts us on a path leading to exaltation in the highest heaven of the celestial world. It is in that highest realm of glory and dignity and honor hereafter that the family unit continues. Those who inherit a place in the highest heaven receive the reward that is named eternal life. Baptism is a gate; celestial marriage is a gate. When we get on the paths of which I speak, we are then obligated to keep the commandments. My suggestion in this field is that you go to the temple and listen to a ceremony of celestial marriage, paying particular and especial attention to the words, and learn what the promises are that are given. And you will learn that all of the promises given are conditioned upon subsequent compliance with all of the terms and conditions of that order of matrimony.

Heresy four: There are those who believe that the doctrine of salvation for the dead offers men a second chance for salvation.

I knew a man, now deceased, not a member of the Church, who was a degenerate old reprobate who found pleasure, as he supposed, in living after the manner of the world. A cigarette dangled from his lips, alcohol stenched his breath, and profane and bawdy stories defiled his lips. His moral status left much to be desired.

His wife was a member of the Church, as faithful as she could be under the circumstances. One day she said to him, "You know the Church is true; why won't you be baptized?" He replied, "Of course I know the Church is true, but I have no intention of changing my habits in order to join it. I prefer to live the way I do. But that doesn't worry me in the slightest. I know that as soon as I die, you will have someone go to the temple and do the work for me and everything will come out all right in the end anyway."

He died and she had the work done in the temple. We do not sit in judgment and deny vicarious ordinances to people. But what will it profit him?

There is no such thing as a second chance to gain salvation. This life is the time and the day of our probation (see Alma 34:31). "After this day of life, which is given us to prepare for eternity, . . . then cometh the night of darkness wherein there can be no labor performed" (Alma 34:33).

For those who do not have an opportunity to believe and obey the holy word in this life, the first chance to gain salvation will come in the spirit world. If those who hear the word for the first time in the realms ahead are the kind of people who would have accepted the gospel here, had the opportunity been afforded them, they will accept it there. Salvation for the dead is for those whose first chance to gain salvation is in the spirit world.

In the revelation recently added to our canon of holy writ, these words are found:

> *Thus came the voice of the Lord unto me, saying: All who have died without a knowledge of this gospel, who would have received it if they had been permitted to tarry, shall be heirs of the celestial kingdom of God;*
>
> *Also all that shall die henceforth without a knowledge of it, who would have received it with all their hearts, shall be heirs of that kingdom;*
>
> *For I, the Lord, will judge all men according to their works, according to the desire of their hearts.* [D&C 137:7–9]

There is no other promise of salvation than the one recited in that revelation. Those who reject the gospel in this life and then receive it in the spirit world go not to the celestial, but to the terrestrial kingdom.

Heresy five: There are those who say that there is progression from one kingdom to another in the eternal worlds or that lower kingdoms eventually progress to where higher kingdoms once were.

This belief lulls men into a state of carnal security. It causes them to say, "God is so merciful; surely he will save us all eventually; if we do not gain the celestial kingdom now, eventually we will; so why worry?" It lets people live a life of sin here and now with the hope that they will be saved eventually.

The true doctrine is that all men will be resurrected, but they will come forth in the resurrection with different kinds of bodies—some celestial, others terrestrial, others telestial, and some with bodies incapable of standing any degree of glory. The body we receive in the resurrection determines the glory we receive in the kingdoms that are prepared.

Of those in the telestial world it is written: "And they shall be servants of the Most High; but where God and Christ dwell they cannot come, worlds without end" (D&C 76:112).

Of those who had the opportunity to enter into the new and everlasting covenant of marriage in this life and who did not do it, the revelation says:

> *Therefore, when they are out of the world they neither marry nor are given in marriage; but are appointed angels in heaven, which angels are ministering servants, to minister for those who are worthy of a far more, and an exceeding, and an eternal weight of glory.*
>
> *For these angels did not abide my law; therefore, they cannot be enlarged, but remain separately and singly, without exaltation, in their saved condition, to all eternity; and from henceforth are not gods, but are angels of God forever and ever.* [D&C 132:16–17]

They neither progress from one kingdom to another, nor does a lower kingdom ever get where a higher kingdom once was. Whatever eternal progression there is, it is within a sphere.

Heresy six: There are those who believe or say they believe that Adam is our father and our god, that he is the father of our spirits and our bodies, and that he is the one we worship.

The devil keeps this heresy alive as a means of obtaining converts to cultism. It is contrary to the whole plan of salvation set forth in the scriptures, and anyone who has read the Book of Moses, and anyone who has received the temple endowment, has no excuse whatever for being led astray by it. Those who are so ensnared reject the living prophet and close their ears to the apostles of their day. "We will follow those who went before," they say. And having so determined, they soon are ready to enter polygamous relationships that destroy their souls.

We worship the Father, in the name of the Son, by the power of the Holy Ghost; and Adam is their foremost servant, by whom the peopling of our planet was commenced.

Heresy seven: There are those who believe we must be perfect to gain salvation.

This is not really a great heresy, only a doctrinal misunderstanding that I mention here in order to help round out our discussion and to turn our attention from negative to positive things. If we keep two principles in mind we will thereby know that good and faithful members of the Church will be saved, even though they are far from perfect in this life.

These two principles are (1) that this life is the appointed time for men to prepare to meet God—this life is the day of our probation; and (2) that the same spirit which possesses our bodies at the time we go out of this mortal life shall have power to possess our bodies in that eternal world (see Alma 34:32, 34).

What we are doing as members of the Church is charting a course leading to eternal life. There was only one perfect being, the Lord Jesus. If men had to be perfect and live all of the law strictly, wholly, and completely, there would be only one saved person in eternity. The prophet taught that there are many things to be done, even beyond the grave, in working out our salvation.

And so what we do in this life is chart a course leading to eternal life. That course begins here and now and continues in the realms ahead. We must determine in our hearts and in our souls, with all the power and ability we have, that from this time forward we will press on in righteousness; by so doing we can go where God and Christ are. If we make that firm determination, and are in the course of our duty when this life is over, we will continue in that course in eternity. That same spirit that possesses our bodies at the time we depart from this mortal life will have power to possess our bodies in the eternal world. If we go out of this life loving the Lord, desiring righteousness, and seeking to acquire the attributes of godliness, we will have that same spirit in the eternal world, and we will then continue to advance and progress until an ultimate, destined day when we will possess, receive, and inherit all things.

Now I do not say these are the only great heresies that prevail among us. There are others that might be mentioned. My suggestion, relative to all doctrines and all principles, is that we become students of holy writ, and that we conform our thinking and our beliefs to what is found in the standard works. We need to be less concerned about the views and opinions that others have expressed and drink directly from the fountain the Lord has given us. Then we shall come to a true understanding of the points of his doctrine. And if we pursue such a course, we will soon find that it proceeds in a different direction than the one that the world pursues. We will not be troubled with the intellectual views and expressions of uninspired people. We will soon obtain for ourselves the witness of the Spirit that we are pursuing a course that is pleasing to the Lord, and this knowledge will have a cleansing and sanctifying and edifying influence upon us.

Now, in order to have things in perspective, let me identify the three greatest heresies in all Christendom. They do not prevail among us, fortunately, but they are part of the gross and universal darkness that covers the earth and blots out from the minds of men those truths upon which salvation rests.

The greatest truth known to man is that there is a God in heaven who is infinite and eternal; that he is the creator, upholder, and preserver of all things; that he created us and the sidereal heavens and ordained and established a plan of salvation whereby we might advance and progress and become like him. The truth pertaining to him is that he is our Father in heaven, that he has a body of flesh and bones as tangible as man's, that he is a literal person, and that if we believe and obey his laws we can gain the exaltation that he possesses. Now that is the greatest truth and the most glorious concept known to the human mind, and the reverse of it is the greatest heresy in all Christendom.

The Christian heresy, where God is concerned, is that Deity is a spirit essence that fills the immensity of space; that he is three beings in one; that he is uncreated, incorporeal, and incomprehensible; that he is without body, parts, or passions; that he is a spirit nothingness that is everywhere and nowhere in particular present. These are concepts written in the creeds had in the churches of the world.

The second greatest truth in all eternity pertains to the divine sonship of the Lord, Jesus Christ. It includes the eternal verity that he was foreordained in the councils of eternity to come to earth and be the redeemer of men, to come and ransom men from the temporal and spiritual death brought upon them by the fall of Adam. This second greatest truth is that Christ worked out the infinite and eternal atoning sacrifice because of which all men are raised in immortality and those who believe and obey are raised also unto eternal life.

Now the second greatest heresy in all Christendom is designed to destroy the glories and wonders of the infinite and eternal atonement. It is that men are saved by some kind of lip service, by the grace of God, without work and without effort on their part.

The third greatest truth known to mankind is that the Holy Spirit of God is a revelator and a sanctifier, that he is a personage of spirit, that his assigned ministry and work in the eternal Godhead is to bear record of the Father and of the Son, to reveal them and their truths to men. His work is to cleanse and perfect human souls, to burn dross and evil out of human souls as though by fire. We call that the baptism of fire.

Now the opposite of that is the third greatest heresy in all Christendom. It is that revelation has ceased, that God's mouth is closed, that the Holy Ghost no longer inspires men, that the gifts of the Spirit were done away with after the death of the ancient apostles, and that we no longer need to follow the course they charted.

I simply name these things; I think you will want to weigh and evaluate what is involved. I think you will want to ponder and wonder and search the scriptures. After Jesus had been teaching the Nephites as a resurrected person, giving them as much truth as in his wisdom he felt they could absorb at one time, he counseled them to go to their homes and to ponder in their hearts the things he had said, and to pray to the Father in his name to find out if they were true, and then to come again on the morrow and he would teach them more.

Now that gives us the pattern by which we should operate in the Church. We come together in congregations, seeking the guidance of the Holy Spirit, studying the revelations, reading the scriptures, and hearing expressions of doctrine and counsel given by those who are appointed. These teachings ought to be delivered by the power of the Holy Spirit. They ought to be received by the same power. And if they are, then the speaker and the hearer will be mutually edified, and we will have true and proper worship.

Then when the meeting is over, the "amen" should not end it. We should go to our homes and to our families and to our circles, and we should search out the revelations and find out what the Lord has said on the subjects involved. We should seek to get in tune with the Holy Spirit and to gain a witness, not solely of the truth and divinity of the work in which we are engaged but also of the doctrines that are taught by those who preach to us. We come into these congregations, and sometimes a speaker brings a jug of living water that has in it many gallons. And when he pours it out on the congregation, all that the members have brought is a single cup and so that's all they take away. Or maybe they have their hands over the cups, and they don't get anything to speak of.

On other occasions we have meetings where the speaker comes and all he brings is a little cup of eternal truth, and the members of the congregation come with a large jug, and all they get in their jugs is the little dribble that came from a man who should have known better and who should have prepared himself and talked from the revelations and spoken by the power of the Holy Spirit. We are obligated in the Church to speak by the power of the Spirit. We are commanded to treasure up the words of light and truth and then give forth the portion that is appropriate and needful on every occasion.

I do not think that the heresies I have named are common in the Church. I think that the great majority of the members of the Church believe and understand true doctrines and seek to apply true principles in their lives. Unfortunately, there are a few people who agitate and stir these matters up, who have some personal ax to grind, and who desire to spread philosophies of their own, philosophies that, as near as the judges in Israel can discern, are not in harmony with the mind and will and purpose of the Lord. It is incumbent upon us to believe the truth. We have the obligation to find out what is truth, and then we have the obligation to walk in the light and to apply the truths that we have learned to ourselves and to influence others to do likewise.

Now the glorious and wondrous thing about this whole system of revealed religion that the Lord, our God, has given us is the fact that it is true. There isn't a grander, a more glorious, a more wondrous concept than the simple one that the work in which we are engaged is true. And because it is true it will triumph and prevail, and the knowledge of God and his truths will roll forth until it covers the whole earth as the waters cover the sea. We do not expect to have a perfect society among us until the millennial day dawns. But that is not far distant. And when that day comes, we will all, as the scriptures say, see eye to eye and speak with one voice, and the Lord himself will dwell among us. He could not dwell among us now because we are divided and we are not living in that perfect harmony and unity and with that devotion that prevailed among the Saints in the city of Enoch.

God grant that we may be wise in what we do, that we may seek truth, that we may live in harmony with the truth, that we may bear testimony of the truth, and that we may, as a consequence, have joy and peace and happiness here and now and be inheritors, in due course, of eternal reward in our Father's kingdom. This is my prayer for myself and for all of you, and for all of the members of the Church, and for honest truthseekers everywhere, and I offer it in the name of the Lord Jesus Christ. Amen.

The Three Pillars of Eternity

Bruce R. McConkie

I know, as do we all, that the things of God can be understood only by the power of the Holy Spirit. And I pray that we may receive a mighty outpouring of that Spirit as we consider the three pillars of eternity—the three great eternal verities upon which salvation rests.

My purpose is to take the three greatest events that have ever occurred in all eternity and show how they are interwoven to form one grand plan of salvation.

If we can gain an understanding of them, then the whole eternal scheme of things will fall into place, and we will be in a position to work out our salvation. If we do not build our house of salvation on a true foundation, we will never make the spiritual progress that will prepare us to enter the Eternal Presence.

THREE GREAT EVENTS

The three pillars of eternity, the three events, preeminent and transcendent above all others, are the creation, the fall, and the atonement. These three are the foundations upon which all things rest. Without any one of them all things would lose their purpose and meaning, and the plans and designs of Deity would come to naught.

This devotional address was given at Brigham Young University on 17 February 1981.

If there had been no creation, we would not be, neither the earth, nor any form of life upon its face. All things, all the primal elements, would be without form and void. God would have no spirit children; there would be no mortal probation; and none of us would be on the way to immortality and eternal life.

If there had been no fall of man, there would not be a mortal probation. Mortal man would not be, nor would there be animals or fowls or fishes or life of any sort upon the earth. And, we repeat, none of us would be on the way to immortality and eternal life.

If there had been no atonement of Christ, all things would be lost. The purposes of creation would vanish away. Lucifer would triumph over men and become the captain of their souls. And, we say it again, none of us would be on the way to immortality and eternal life.

And so I now say: Come and let us reason together; let us reason as did righteous men of old that we may come to understanding.

Come and hear us declare sound doctrine; let us declare it plainly and in power as do the angels of God in heaven.

Come and let us testify of those things which God has made known to us; let us testify as do those whose souls are afire with the Spirit and who know by revelation of the truth and verity of their spoken word.

THE ATONEMENT

Let us gaze first at a scene of sorrow and suffering in a garden called Gethsemane, the garden of the oil press. There, outside Jerusalem's walls, on the now sacred side of Olivet, we see eight of the Twelve huddled at the garden gate. Inside the garden are Peter, James, and John. It is night, and the eyes of all are heavy with sleep.

About a stone's cast removed from the three we see the Son of God in sorrow and agony beyond compare. He has fallen on his face. We hear his pleading words: "O my Father, if it be possible, let this cup pass from me: nevertheless not as I will, but as thou wilt" (Matthew 26:39).

We see great gouts of blood drop from every pore. An angel—surely it is mighty Michael himself—comes down from heaven and strengthens him. He trembles because of pain and suffers in both body and spirit. He comes off triumphant; and in a way incomprehensible to us, he bears the sins of all men on conditions of repentance.

Now let our gaze turn to Golgotha. There, at the place of a skull, we see him again, crucified between two thieves. It is noon, and his mangled and scourged body has already hung on that accursed tree for some three hours.

Again it is the hour of atonement. The sun is darkened; for three long hours there is "darkness over all the earth" (Luke 23:44), as all the agonies and sufferings of Gethsemane return. Then the victory is won; the ransom is paid; the atonement is accomplished.

Some thirty-eight or forty hours later—after three days as the Jews counted time—we see him by a garden tomb. He has risen in glorious immortality. Clothed with immortality and eternal life, he gently restrains one of the beloved Marys from embracing him with the same intimacy that had once prevailed.

Soon angelic choirs will fill the heavens as the redeemed sing, "Worthy is the Lamb that was slain to receive power, and riches, and wisdom, and strength, and honour, and glory, and blessing" (Revelation 5:12).

And thus it is that salvation is in Christ, that his atoning sacrifice is the heart and core and center of revealed religion, and that he—in Gethsemane of sorrowful memory and on the cross of Calvary—put into full operation all the terms and conditions of his Father's plan.

He is the resurrection and the life. He is the Redeemer of the world and the Savior of men. He "hath abolished death, and hath brought life and immortality to light through the gospel" (2 Timothy 1:10). It was his work and his glory "to bring to pass the immortality and eternal life of man" (Moses 1:39). And his is the only name given under heaven whereby man may be saved.

If there had been no atonement of Christ, there would be no resurrection, no breaking of the bands of death, no coming forth from the grave.

If there had been no atonement, there would be no remission of sins; no return to the presence of God; no salvation of any sort, kind, or nature; no eternal life; no exaltation; no continuation of the family unit in eternity.

If there were no atonement of Christ, all men would be subject to "that awful monster the devil, and death, and hell, and that lake of fire and brimstone, which is endless torment" (2 Nephi 9:19).

If there were no atonement of Christ, "our spirits" would have become "like unto" Lucifer's, "and we become devils, angels to a devil, to be shut out from the presence of our God, and to remain with the father of lies, in misery, like unto himself" (2 Nephi 9:9).

If there were no atonement of Christ, all men would be damned everlastingly, all would be sons of perdition, and the whole purpose of God and his eternal plan of salvation would utterly fail.

All things center in, revolve around, are anchored to, and are built upon the atoning sacrifice of the Lord Jesus Christ. There is no language given to men or angels to proclaim these truths with the power and verity and dignity that should attend them. Let it be blazoned in burning fire through all the sidereal heavens that salvation is in Christ and comes because of his atoning sacrifice.

Now this atoning sacrifice of the Lord Jesus Christ—grand and infinite, glorious and eternal as it is—does not stand alone. It is not simply a sudden blaze of light in a universe of darkness and despair. It is not by itself alone a great sun rising in celestial splendor to dispel the gloom of endless night. It is not merely a manifestation of the grace of an infinite God toward his fallen children.

However much the atonement may be and is all these things— and more!—yet it does not stand alone. It is not a child born without parents. It has roots; it has a reason for being; it came because other events called it forth.

THE FALL

The atonement is part of the eternal plan of the Father. It came at the appointed time, according to the will of the Father, to do for man that which could not have been done in any other way. The atonement is the child of the fall, and the fall is the father of the atonement. Neither of them, without the other, could have brought to pass the eternal purposes of the Father.

The fall of Adam and the atonement of Christ are linked together—inseparably, everlastingly, never to be parted. They are as much a part of the same body as are the head and the heart, and each plays its part in the eternal scheme of things.

The fall of Adam brought temporal and spiritual death into the world, and the atonement of Christ ransomed men from these two deaths by bringing to pass the immortality and eternal life of man. This makes the fall as essential a part of the plan of salvation as the very atonement itself.

There are, in fact, five things that came into being and continue to exist because of the fall. None of these things would have existed if there had been no fall, and all of them are essential parts of the divine plan of salvation. They are:

1. *Temporal death.* This is the natural death; it occurs when body and spirit separate; it results in corruption and decay. Because of the atonement of Christ all men will be raised from corruption to incorruption, from mortality to immortality, thence to live everlastingly in a resurrected state.

2. *Spiritual death.* This is death as pertaining to the things of the Spirit. It is death as pertaining to things of righteousness. It is to be cast out of the presence of the Lord. It is a way of life which is in opposition to that of the Father of us all. Because of the atonement, because the Lord Jesus bore our sins on conditions of repentance, we have power to gain eternal life, which is spiritual life, which is a life of righteousness, which is life in the presence of our God.

3. *Mortality.* Mortal life comes because of the fall. If there had been no fall, there would be no mortal life of any sort on earth. Mortal life is life where there is death. Death must enter the world to bring mortality into being.

4. *Procreation.* Before the fall there was no procreation. I repeat, for thus saith the Holy Word, before the fall there was no procreation. Adam and Eve, in their Edenic state, could not have

children, nor, as we shall see, could any form of life when first placed on the newly created paradisiacal earth.

5. *A probationary estate.* We are here to be tried and tested, to see if we will believe the truths of salvation and keep the commandments while we walk by faith. After the fall men became carnal, sensual, and devilish by nature, and the plan of salvation calls upon them to put off these worldly snares and to put on Christ.

Now, lest there be any sliver of misunderstanding about any of this, let us reason together on all these things as did they of old. Indeed, let us use the very words they used as they are found in the holy scriptures.

"Now is Christ risen from the dead," Paul said as he testified of the atonement. "For since by man came death, by man came also the resurrection of the dead." Adam brought death, and if he had not fallen there would be no death; and Christ brought the resurrection, and, if there had been no atonement, there would be no resurrection. "For as in Adam all die, even so in Christ shall all be made alive" (1 Corinthians 15:20–22).

Moroni linked the fall and the atonement together in this way. God, he said, "created Adam, and by Adam came the fall of man. And because of the fall of man came Jesus Christ." It is just that simple; the fall is the source and cause and reason for the atonement. "And because of Jesus Christ came the redemption of man" (Mormon 9:12). Salvation is in Christ!

"And because of the redemption of man, which came by Jesus Christ," men "are brought back into the presence of the Lord; yea, this is wherein all men are redeemed, because the death of Christ bringeth to pass the resurrection, which bringeth to pass a redemption from an endless sleep" (Mormon 9:13).

What did the angel say to King Benjamin? He said, Christ's "blood atoneth for the sins of those who have fallen by the transgression of Adam" (Mosiah 3:11). We are descendants of Adam; we all have a common father.

He said, "As in Adam, or by nature, they fall, even so the blood of Christ atoneth for their sins" (Mosiah 3:16). The blessings of the fall have passed upon all men; all can be redeemed because Adam fell and Christ came.

He said, "Salvation was, and is, and is to come, in and through the atoning blood of Christ, the Lord Omnipotent" (Mosiah 3:18). There is no other source of salvation from the fall than that which comes through Christ.

He said, "The natural man is an enemy to God, and has been from the fall of Adam, and will be, forever and ever, unless he yields to the enticings of the Holy Spirit, and putteth off the natural man and becometh a saint through the atonement of Christ the Lord" (Mosiah 3:19).

Thus the natural man, which is Adam, is conquered by the perfect man, which is Christ; and thus "all mankind may be saved, by obedience to the laws and ordinances of the Gospel" (Articles of Faith 1:3). And now, what saith our great and good friend Lehi about all these things?

He saith that the Redeemer "cometh to bring salvation unto men. . . . And the way is prepared [for him] from the fall of man, and salvation is free" (2 Nephi 2:3–4). The fall is the foundation upon which the atonement rests.

He saith that "after Adam and Eve had partaken of the forbidden fruit they were driven out of the garden of Eden, to till the earth" (2 Nephi 2:19). Their mortal probation and the trials and tests of mortality began after the fall.

He saith:

And they have brought forth children; yea, even the family of all the earth. [2 Nephi 2:20]

Every living soul on earth is a descendant of Adam and Eve. God hath made of one blood all the nations of men.

He saith:

If Adam had not transgressed he would not have fallen, but he would have remained in the garden of Eden. [2 Nephi 2:22]

If Adam had not fallen, he would be there today, six thousand years later, in all the glory and beauty of his immortal nature. Such is the word of holy writ.

And next—marvel of marvels and wonder of wonders—Lehi saith, "And all things which were created"—*all things* means all things; it includes animals and fishes and fowls and creeping things and plants; it includes dinosaurs and whales and ants; it means all things—

All things which were created must have remained in the same state in which they were after they were created; and they must have remained forever, and had no end. [2 Nephi 2:22]

There was, we repeat, no death in the world until after Adam fell. And there was, we repeat, no procreation until after the fall. And there was, we repeat, no mortality until after the fall.

And so Lehi continues, "And they"—Adam and Eve—"would have had no children" (2 Nephi 2:23).

And then, on the foundation so laid, while filled with light and guided by the Spirit, Lehi acclaimed:

Adam fell that men might be; and men are, that they might have joy.
And the Messiah cometh in the fulness of time, that he may redeem the children of men from the fall. [2 Nephi 2:25–26]

Truly, as Enoch said:

Because that Adam fell, we are; and by his fall came death; and we are made partakers of misery and woe. . . .
And men have become carnal, sensual, and devilish, and are shut out from the presence of God. [Moses 6:48, 49]

Truly, as Mother Eve said:

Were it not for our transgression we never should have had seed, and never should have known good and evil, and the joy of our redemption, and the eternal life which God giveth to all the obedient. [Moses 5:11]

Truly, salvation comes because of the fall, and it is just as important to believe in the fall as it is to believe in the atonement, and, indeed, it is not possible to believe in the atonement without believing in the fall.

THE CREATION

Now, even as the atonement grows out of the fall, so the fall grows out of the creation. If all things had not been created in the very way in which they were created, there could have been no fall. If created things were to fall, they must be created in a higher state than the state they would be in after the fall. To fall is to go downward or forward, not upward.

And so it is that the revealed accounts of the creation of this earth and all things on the face thereof are accounts of the paradisiacal creation. They speak of the immortal state in which all things were first made; they are telling of created things in the day before death entered the world.

Our tenth Article of Faith says: "We believe . . . that the earth will be renewed and receive its paradisiacal glory." When the Lord comes and the millennial era commences, there will be new heavens and a new earth; the earth will be renewed; it will become new again; and it will return to its paradisiacal state; it will become as it was in the Edenic day. And once again death as we know it will cease.

The accounts of the creation in Genesis 1 and Moses 2 are accounts of the paradisiacal or Edenic creation. They are descriptive of a creation that antedated death and mortality and the fall. They speak of a creation in which—again these are Lehi's words—

All things which were created must have remained in the same state in which they were after they were created; and they must have remained forever, and had no end. [2 Nephi 2:22]

That is, they would have so remained if there had been no fall.

RECAPITULATION

Now, we are speaking of the three pillars of heaven, of the three greatest events ever to occur in all eternity, of the three doctrines that are woven inseparably together to form the plan of salvation. We are speaking of the creation, the fall, and the atonement. And these things are one. And, be it noted, all things were created; all things fell; and all things are subject to the redeeming power of the Son of God.

I am not conscious of expressing a single thought or concept that has not already been said by the Brethren who have gone before. Almost every sentence I have uttered is a quotation or a paraphrase of something said by Joseph Smith, Brigham Young, John Taylor, Joseph F. Smith, Joseph Fielding Smith, Orson Pratt, or some other of the great theologians of our dispensation.

Many among us have no difficulty envisioning that the atonement is infinite and eternal and applies to all forms of life. They know that the revelations say in so many words that all forms of life both lived as spirit entities and will be resurrected—animals, fowls, fishes—all things are eternal in nature.

But some among us have not yet had it dawn upon them that all things fell and became mortal so they could be resurrected.

The early Brethren of our dispensation wrote these words:

The word atonement signifies deliverance, through the offering of a ransom, from the penalty of a broken law. . . . As effected by Jesus Christ, it signifies the deliverance, through his death and resurrection, of the earth and everything pertaining to it, from the power which death has obtained over them through the transgression of Adam. . . . Redemption from death, through the sufferings of Christ, is for all men, both the righteous and the wicked; for this earth, and for all things created upon it. [*Compendium*, pp. 8–9, cited in *Mormon Doctrine*, Bruce R. McConkie (Salt Lake City: Bookcraft, 1966), pp. 64–65.]

THREE GLORIOUS BEINGS

When we speak of the creation, the fall, and the atonement, we are speaking of the works of Elohim, Jehovah, and Michael. We are talking of the doctrines which are stated or are implicit in our first three Articles of Faith. We need to come to a unity of faith as to the labors of each of these glorious beings.

Who is Elohim? He is God the Eternal Father. He is a glorified and exalted personage. He "has a body of flesh and bones as tangible as man's" (D&C 130:22). In the language of Adam, Man of Holiness is his name. He is omnipotent, omniscient, and omnipresent. He knows all things and has all power—not simply as pertaining to us or in some prescribed sphere or realm—but in the absolute, eternal, and unlimited sense. In the ultimate sense, he is the Creator. And anything you may have heard to the contrary, whether in the creeds of Christendom or the mouthings of intellectuals who, in their own eyes, know more than the Lord, is false.

Who is Michael? He is a spirit son of the great Elohim. Under Christ he led the armies of righteousness when there was war in heaven. Our revelations say that he "was the son of God" (Moses 6:22), that he was "the first flesh [the first mortal flesh] upon the earth, the first man also" (Moses 3:7), and that he was "the first man of all men" (Moses 1:34). He is Adam, our father; he is the presiding high priest over all the earth. Under Christ, who is "the Holy One," he holds "the keys of salvation" (D&C 78:16). He is the only one by whom the fall came. And anything you may have heard to the contrary, from whatever source, is false.

Who is Jehovah? He is the Lord Jesus Christ, the Firstborn of the Father, the Savior and Redeemer. He is the Lamb slain from the foundation of the world. He is the Only Begotten in the flesh, the only person ever born with a mortal mother and an immortal Father. He worked out the infinite and eternal atonement, ransomed men and all forms of life from the fall, and made the purposes of creation operative. Salvation is in him and comes to those who believe and obey. And anything you may have heard to the contrary is false.

The truths relative to Elohim, Jehovah, and Michael are the greatest of all eternal verities. They wrap the creation, the fall, and the atonement into one grand plan of salvation. They are the gospel of God who is the Father. And of their truth the Holy Ghost bears witness.

God grant that we may all believe and know and understand the great eternal verities by which salvation comes and that, believing and knowing and understanding, we may so live as to gain eternal life. In the name of Jesus Christ. Amen.

What Think Ye
of Salvation by Grace?

Bruce R. McConkie

I think I'll take as a text what we just sang:

Glory to God on high!
Let heav'n and earth reply.
Praise ye his name.
His love and grace adore,
Who all our sorrows bore.
Sing aloud evermore:
Worthy the Lamb!
[James Allen, "Glory to God on High," *Hymns* no. 67]

I wonder how many of us are aware of one of the great religious phenomena of the ages, one that is now sweeping through Protestant Christianity, as only one other thing has ever done in the whole Christian Era.

We are silent witnesses of an almost worldwide religious craze that had its birth in the minds of a few great religious reformers

This devotional address was given at Brigham Young University on 10 January 1984.

nearly five hundred years ago and which is now receiving a new birth of freedom and influence.

May I divorce myself for a moment from the mainstream of present-day evangelical Christianity, swim upstream as it were, and give forth some rather plain and pointed expression on this supposedly marvelous means of being saved with very slight effort.

THE ORIGINAL HERESY

But before zeroing in on this religious mania that has now taken possession of millions of devout but deluded people, and as a means of keeping all things in perspective, let me first identify the original heresy that did more than anything else to destroy the primitive Christianity.

This first and chief heresy of a now fallen and decadent Christianity—and truly it is the father of all heresies—swept through all of the congregations of true believers in the early centuries of the Christian Era; it pertained then and pertains now to the nature and kind of being that God is.

It was the doctrine, adapted from Gnosticism, that changed Christianity from the religion in which men worshipped a personal God, in whose image man is made, into the religion in which men worshipped a spirit essence called the Trinity. This new God, no longer a personal Father, no longer a personage of tabernacle, became an incomprehensible three-in-one spirit essence that filled the immensity of space.

The adoption of this false doctrine about God effectively destroyed the true worship among men and ushered in the age of universal apostasy. The dominant church then became a political power, ruling autocratically over kingdoms and empires as well as over her own congregations. Salvation, as was then supposed, was administered by the church through the seven sacraments.

THE SECOND GREATEST HERESY

Nearly a millennium and a half later, during the sixteenth century, as the Reformation grew out of the Renaissance, as a means of breaking the hold of the dominant church, the great Christian reformers lit a new doctrinal fire. That fire, burning wildly over the dry and arid prairies of religious autocracy, is what really prepared the way for the restoration of the gospel in modern times.

It was nonetheless the doctrinal fire—the burning, flaming, heretical fire—that became the second greatest heresy of Christendom, because it effectively destroyed the efficacy and power of the atonement of the Lord Jesus Christ by whom salvation comes.

The first great heresy, sweeping like a prairie fire through the struggling branches of a newly born Christianity, destroyed the worship of the true God. And the second, a heresy originating in the same courts of darkness, destroyed that very atonement of God's only Son.

This second heresy—and it is the delusion and mania that prevails to this day in the great evangelical body of Protestantism— is the doctrine that we are justified by faith alone, without the works of the law. It is the doctrine that we are saved by grace alone, without works. It is the doctrine that we may be born again simply by confessing the Lord Jesus with our lips while we continue to live in our sins.

We have all listened to sermons by the great revivalists and self-appointed prophets of the various radio and television ministries. Whatever the subjects of their sermons may be, they always end with an invitation and a plea for people to come forward and confess the Lord Jesus and receive the cleansing power of his blood.

Television broadcasts of these sermons always show arenas or coliseums or stadiums filled with people, scores and hundreds and thousands of whom go forward to make their confessions, to become born-again Christians, to be saved with all they suppose this includes.

While driving along a highway in my car, I was listening to the radio sermon of one of these evangelists who was preaching of salvation by grace alone. He said all anyone had to do to be saved was to believe in Christ and perform an affirmative act of confession.

Among other things he said: "If you are traveling in a car, simply reach forth your hand and touch your car radio, thus making contact with me, and then say, 'Lord Jesus, I believe,' and you will be saved."

Unfortunately, I did not accept his generous invitation to gain instant salvation; and so I suppose my opportunity is lost forever! Interwoven with this concept is the doctrine that the elect of God are predestined to be saved regardless of any act on their part, which, as I suppose, is part of the reason a Lutheran minister once said to me: "I was saved two thousand years ago, and there is nothing I can do about it one way or the other now," meaning that he thought he was saved by the blood of Christ shed on Calvary, without any works or effort on his part.

THE EXAMPLE OF MARTIN LUTHER

Here is an account of how Martin Luther himself came to believe the doctrine of justification by faith alone; it is an ideal illustration of why this doctrine has such wide appeal.

A friendly biographer tells us: Luther "was much concerned about his personal salvation and given to gloomy reflections over his sinful condition," so much so that "he fell dangerously ill, and was seized with a fit of despair." Also:

> No one surpassed him in prayer, fasting, night watches, self-mortification. He was . . . a model of sanctity. But . . . he found no peace and rest in all his pious exercises. . . . He saw sin everywhere. . . . He could not trust in God as a reconciled Father, as a God of love and mercy, but trembled before him, as a God of wrath, as a consuming fire. . . . It was sin as an all-pervading power and vitiating principle, sin as a corruption of nature, sin as an alienation from God and hostility to God that weighed on his mind like an incubus and brought him to the brink of despair.

While in this state, he gained

> the conviction that the sinner is justified by faith alone, without the works of the law. . . . This experience acted like a new revelation on Luther. It shed light upon the whole Bible and made it to him a book of life and comfort. He felt relieved of the terrible load of guilt by an act of free grace. He was led out of the dark prison house of self-inflicted penance into the daylight and

fresh air of God's redeeming love. Justification broke the fetters of legalistic slavery, and filled him with the joy and peace of the state of adoption; it opened to him the very gates of heaven. [Philip Schaff, *History of the Christian Church,* vol. 7, pp. 111, 116–17, 122–24]

So says Luther's biographer.

It should be perfectly clear to all of us that Luther's break with Catholicism was part of the divine program; it came as an Elias preparing the way for the Restoration. But this does not in any sense put a stamp of divine approval on the doctrine he devised to justify the break in his own mind.

A MODERN-DAY EXAMPLE

I received a letter from a returned missionary whom I shall call Elder Carnalus Luciferno, for no one in his right mind would have such a name, and my correspondent was certainly out of his mind.

His letter told me of his own conversion, of his service as a zone leader in the mission field, and of making many converts. But after returning home, as he expressed it, "I returned to my old Gentile ways."

After thus ceasing to be a true Saint, and becoming a genuine Gentile, he met some representatives of another church who taught him that we are saved by grace, without works, simply by believing in the Lord Jesus.

Thereupon he was saved, and his letter, which he sent to many people, was an invitation to these others to believe in Christ and be saved as he was saved.

Later I said to his mission president, "Tell me about Elder Carnalus Luciferno."

"Oh," he said, "Elder Carnalus Luciferno was a good missionary who made many converts. But since returning home he has been excommunicated."

"Oh," I said. "What was his problem?"

The mission president replied, "Before he joined the Church, he was a homosexual, and we understood that since his release he has reverted to his old ways."

THE STRAIT AND NARROW WAY

Now, let us reason together on this matter of being saved without the need to do the works of righteousness. Did you ever wonder why our missionaries convert one of a city and two of a family while the preachers of this doctrine of salvation by grace alone gain millions of converts?

Does it seem strange to you that we wear out our lives in bringing one soul unto Christ, that we may have joy with him in the kingdom of the Father, while our evangelist colleagues cannot even count their converts, so great is their number?

Why are those who come to hear the message of the Restoration numbered in the hundreds *and* thousands, rather than in the hundreds *of* thousands?

May I suggest that the difference is between the strait and narrow way, which few find, and the broad way "that leadeth to destruction, and many there be which go in thereat" (Matthew 7:13–14).

All men must have and do have some way of worship—call it what you will—be it Christianity or Communism or Buddhism or athe-ism, or the wandering ways of Islam. I repeat: All men must and do worship; this inclination is given them by their Creator as a natural gift and endowment. The Light of Christ is shed forth upon all man-kind; all men have a conscience and know by instinct the difference between good and evil; it is inherent in the human personality to seek and worship a divine being of some sort.

As we are aware, since the Fall all men have become carnal, sensual, and devilish by nature; they have become worldly; and their inclination is to live after the manner of the flesh and satisfy their lusts and appetites.

Accordingly, anytime men can devise a system of worship that will let them continue to live after the manner of the world, to live in their carnal and fallen state, and at the same time one which will satisfy their innate and instinctive desires to worship, such, to them, is a marvelous achievement.

SALVATION BY GRACE

Now, there is a true doctrine of salvation by grace—a salvation by grace alone and without works, as the scriptures say. To understand this doctrine we must define our terms as they are defined in holy writ.

1. What is salvation? It is both immortality and eternal life. It is an inheritance in the highest heaven of the celestial world. It consists of the fullness of the glory of the Father and is reserved for those for whom the family unit continues in eternity. Those who are saved become as God is and live as he lives.

2. What is the plan of salvation? It is the system ordained by the Father to enable his spirit children to advance and progress and become like him. It consists of three great and eternal verities—the Creation, the Fall, and the Atonement—without any of which there could be no salvation.

3. What is the grace of God? It is his mercy, his love, and his condescension—all manifest for the benefit and blessing of his children, all operating to bring to pass the immortality and eternal life of man.

We rejoice in the heavenly condescension that enabled Mary to become "the mother of the Son of God, after the manner of the flesh" (1 Nephi 11:18).

We bask in the eternal love that sent the Only Begotten into the world "that whosoever believeth in him should not perish, but have everlasting life" (John 3:16).

We are profoundly grateful for that mercy which endureth forever and through which salvation is offered to erring mortals.

4. Does salvation come by grace, or grace alone, by grace without works? It surely does, without any question in all its parts, types, kinds, and degrees.

We are saved by grace, without works; it is a gift of God. How else could it come?

In his goodness and grace the great God ordained and established the plan of salvation. No works on our part were required.

In his goodness and grace he created this earth and all that is on it, with man as the crowning creature of his creating—without which creation his spirit children could not obtain immortality and eternal life. No works on our part were required.

In his goodness and grace he provided for the Fall of man, thus bringing mortality and death and a probationary estate into being—without all of which there would be no immortality and eternal life. And again no works on our part were required.

In his goodness and grace—and this above all—he gave his Only Begotten Son to ransom man and all life from the temporal and spiritual death brought into the world by the Fall of Adam.

He sent his Son to redeem mankind, to atone for the sins of the world, "to bring to pass the immortality and eternal life of man" (Moses 1:39). And again all this comes to us as a free gift and without works.

There is nothing any man could do to create himself. This was the work of the Lord God.

Nor did we have any part in the Fall of man, without which there could be no salvation. The Lord provided the way, and Adam and Even put the system into operation.

And finally, there neither has been, nor is, nor ever can be any way nor means by which man alone can, or any power he possesses, redeem himself.

We cannot resurrect ourselves anymore than we can create ourselves. We cannot create a heavenly abode for the Saints, nor make provision for the continuation of the family unit in eternity, nor bring salvation and exaltation into being. All these things are ordained and established by that God who is the Father of us all. And they all came into being and are made available to us, as free gifts, without works, because of the infinite goodness and grace of Him whose children we are.

Truly, there is no way to overstate the goodness and grandeurs and glories of the grace of God which bringeth salvation. Such wondrous love, such unending mercy, such infinite compassion and condescension—all these can come only from the Eternal God who lives in eternal life and who desires all of his children to live as he lives and be inheritors of eternal life.

TEACHING IN THE EARLY CHURCH

Knowing these things, as did Paul and our fellow apostles of old, let us put ourselves in their position. What words shall we choose to offer to the world the blessings of a freely given atoning sacrifice?

On the one hand, we are preaching to Jews who, in their lost and fallen state, have rejected their Messiah and who believe that they are saved by the works and performances of the Mosaic law.

On the other hand, we are preaching to pagans—Romans, Greeks, those in every nation—who know nothing whatever about the Messianic word, or of the need for a Redeemer, or of the working out of the infinite and eternal atonement. They worship idols, the forces of nature, the heavenly bodies, or whatever suits their fancy. As with the Jews, they assume that this or that sacrifice or appeasing act will please the Deity of their choice and some vague and unspecified blessings will result.

Can either the Jews or the pagans be left to assume that the works they do will save them? Or must they forget their little groveling acts of petty worship, gain faith in Christ, and rely on the cleansing power of his blood for salvation?

They must be taught faith in the Lord Jesus Christ and to forsake their traditions and performances. Surely we must tell them they cannot be saved by the works they are doing, for man cannot save himself. Instead they must turn to Christ and rely on his merits and mercy and grace.

TEACHING BY ABINADI

Abinadi struggled with this same problem in his contentions with the priests and people of Noah. They had the law of Moses, with its various rites and performances, but they knew nothing of the Atoning One. And so Abinadi asked, "Doth salvation come by the law of Moses? What say ye? And they answered and said that salvation did come by the law of Moses" (Mosiah 12:31–32).

After teaching them some of the great truths of salvation, Abinadi answered his own question: "Salvation doth not come by the law alone; and were it not for the atonement, which God himself shall make for the sins and iniquities of his people, that they must unavoidably perish, notwithstanding the law of Moses" (Mosiah 13:28). Salvation is not in works—not even in those revealed of God—but in Christ and his atonement.

MODERN-DAY TEACHING

Now let us suppose a modern-day case. Suppose we have the scriptures, the gospel, the priesthood, the Church, the ordinances, the organization, even the keys of the kingdom—everything that now is down to the last jot and tittle—and yet there is no atonement of Christ. What then? Can we be saved? Will all our good works save us? Will we be rewarded for all our righteousness?

Most assuredly we will not. We are not saved by works alone, no matter how good; we are saved because God sent his Son to shed his blood in Gethsemane and on Calvary "that all thru him might ransomed be" ("'Tis Sweet to Sing the Matchless Love," *Hymns,* no. 176). We are saved by the blood of Christ.

To paraphrase Abinadi: "Salvation doth not come by the Church alone: and were it not for the atonement, given by the grace of God as a free gift, all men must unavoidably perish, and this notwithstanding the Church and all that appertains to it."

Let us now come to the matter of whether we must do something to gain the blessings of the atonement in our lives. And we find the answer written in words of fire and emblazoned across the whole heavens; we hear a voice speaking with the sound of ten thousand trumpets; the very heavens and the earth are moved out of their place, so powerful is the word that goes forth. It is the message that neither men, nor angels, nor the Gods themselves can proclaim with an undue emphasis.

This is the word: Man cannot be saved by grace alone; as the Lord lives, man must keep the commandments; he must work the works of righteousness; he must work out his salvation with fear and trembling before the Lord; he must have faith like the ancients—the faith that brings with it gifts and signs and miracles.

"YE MUST PRESS FORWARD"

Does it suffice to believe and be baptized without more? The answer is no, in every language and tongue. Rather, after belief, after repentance, after baptism,

Ye must press forward with a steadfastness in Christ, having a perfect brightness of hope, and a love of God and of all men. Wherefore, if ye shall press forward, feasting upon the word of Christ, and endure to the end, behold, thus saith the Father: Ye shall have eternal life.

And now, behold, . . . this is the way; and there is none other way nor name given under heaven whereby man can be saved in the kingdom of God. [2 Nephi 31:20–21]

John, the beloved apostle, promises the Saints eternal life with the Father on this condition,

If we walk in the light, as he is in the light, we have fellowship one with another, and the blood of Jesus Christ his Son cleanseth us from all sin. [1 John 1:7]

The blood of Christ was shed as a free gift of wondrous grace, but the Saints are cleansed by the blood after they keep the commandments.

Nowhere has this ever been taught better than in these words of the risen Lord to his Nephite brethren:

And no unclean thing can enter into his kingdom; therefore nothing entereth into his rest save it be those who have washed their garments in my blood, because of their faith, and the repentance of all their sins, and their faithfulness unto the end.

Now this is the commandment: Repent, all ye ends of the earth, and come unto me and be baptized in my name, that ye may be sanctified by

the reception of the Holy Ghost, that ye may stand spotless before me at the last day.

Verily, verily, I say unto you, this is my gospel; and ye know the things that ye must do in my church; for the works which ye have seen me do that shall ye also do; for that which ye have seen me do even that shall ye do;

Therefore, if ye do these things blessed are ye, for ye shall be lifted up at the last day. [3 Nephi 27:19–22]

Men must be "doers of the word, and not hearers only" (James 1:22); they must do the very works that Christ did; and those who have true and saving faith in him accomplish this very end.

OUR DAY'S NEED: CORRECT INTERPRETATION

In our day, among other Christians at least, we are not faced with the problems of our predecessors. They had to show that any works then being performed were of no avail without the atonement, that salvation was in Christ and his spilt blood, and that all men must come unto him to be saved.

Our need in today's world, in which Christians assume there was an atonement, is to interpret the scriptures properly and to call upon men to keep the commandments so as to become worthy of the cleansing power of the blood of the Lamb.

Hear, then, the word of the Lord Jesus:

Not every one that saith unto me, Lord, Lord, shall enter into the kingdom of heaven; but he that doeth the will of my Father which is in heaven. [Matthew 7:21]

And it is the will of the Father—as a thousand scriptures attest—that all men everywhere must endure to the end, must keep the commandments, must work out their salvation with fear and trembling before the Lord, or they can in no wise enter into the kingdom of heaven.

How well Nephi said,

Believe in Christ, and . . . be reconciled to God; for we know that it is by grace that we are saved, after all we can do. [2 Nephi 25:23]

GOSPEL CALL TO RIGHTEOUSNESS

Salvation by grace alone and without works, as it is taught in large segments of Christendom today, is akin to what Lucifer proposed in the preexistence—that he would save all mankind and one soul should not be lost. He would save them without agency, without works, without any act on their part.

As with the proposal of Lucifer in the preexistence to save all mankind, so with the doctrine of salvation by grace alone, without works, as it is taught in modern Christendom—both concepts are false. There is no salvation in either of them. They both come from the same source; they are not of God.

We believe and proclaim that it is life eternal to know the only wise and true God and Jesus Christ whom he has sent (see John 17:3). Let men worship whomsoever they will, but there is no salvation in worshipping any God but the true God.

We believe and proclaim that salvation is in Christ, in his gospel, in his atoning sacrifice. We are bold to say it comes by the goodness and grace of the Father and the Son. No people on earth praise the Lord with greater faith and fervor than we do because of this goodness and grace.

As the Lord's agents, as his servants, as ambassadors of Christ— sent by him, sent to speak in his place instead, sent to say what he would say if he personally were here—we testify that no man, as long as the earth shall stand, or the heavens endure, or God continues as God, no man shall ever be saved in the kingdom of God, in the celestial kingdom of heaven, without doing the works of righteousness.

As far as man is concerned, the great and eternal plan of salvation is:

1. Faith in the Lord Jesus Christ; faith in him as the Son of God; faith in him as the Savior and Redeemer who shed his blood for us in Gethsemane and on Calvary;

2. Repentance of all our sins—thus forsaking the world and its carnal course; thus turning from the broad way that leads to destruction; thus preparing for the spiritual rebirth into the kingdom of God;

3. Baptism by immersion for the remission of sins; baptism under the hands of a legal administrator who has power to bind on earth and seal in heaven—thus planting our feet firmly on the strait and narrow path leading to eternal life;

4. Receiving the gift of the Holy Ghost—thus enabling us to be baptized with fire; to have sin and evil burned out of our souls as though by fire; to be sanctified so as to stand pure and spotless before the Lord at the last day; and

5. Enduring to the end in righteousness, keeping the commandments, and living by every word that proceedeth forth from the mouth of God.

Thus saith the Lord:

He who doeth the works of righteousness shall receive his reward, even peace in this world, and eternal life in the world to come. [D&C 59:23]

As God is true, and Christ is the Savior, and the Holy Ghost is their minister and witness, such is the plan of salvation, and there neither is nor ever shall be any other.

Let those in the world think and act as they please; let us, the Saints of God who know better, together with all who are willing to live by the higher standard of the gospel, praise the Lord for his goodness and grace and do so by keeping his commandments, thereby becoming heirs of eternal salvation.

Glory to God on high!
Let heav'n and earth reply.
Praise ye his name.
His love and grace adore,
Who all our sorrows bore.

Sing aloud evermore:
Worthy the Lamb!
[*Hymns,* no. 67]

In the name of the Lord Jesus Christ. Amen.

The Mystery of Godliness

—◆—

Bruce R. McConkie

I rejoice in the privilege of presenting to the young and rising generation some basic concepts about the deepest and most profound doctrine of the gospel.

It is the first principle of revealed religion, the great cornerstone upon which all else rests, the foundation for all of the doctrines of salvation.

I shall speak of what the revealed word calls the mystery of godliness.

If our vision is blurred where this doctrine and these concepts are concerned, or, if knowingly or unknowingly we have fallen prey to any of the false sectarian notions that abound with reference to them, our progress toward eternal life will be slow indeed.

COMPREHENDING THE MYSTERY OF GODLINESS

A mystery, so the dictionary says, is "something beyond human comprehension." Defining the word from a theological standpoint,

This fireside address was given at Brigham Young University on 6 January 1985.

it says a mystery is "an article of faith beyond human comprehension, as the doctrine of the Trinity."

How apt this illustration is! If there was ever something beyond human comprehension, it is the sectarian doctrine of the Trinity. This doctrine defines God and the Godhead as a three-in-one spirit essence that fills the immensity of space; it teaches that it and they are without body, parts, or passions; it acclaims that it and they are unknown, unknowable, and uncreated, and specifies, in the creeds, that unless we believe all these things we cannot be saved.

It is true that finite man cannot comprehend his Infinite Maker in the full sense of the word. We cannot tell how gods began to be or from whence existent matter came.

But we are duty-bound to learn all that God has revealed about himself and his everlasting gospel. If we are to gain eternal life we must come to know the Great God and his Only Begotten, whom he sent into the world. And this probationary estate is the appointed time to begin to know God, and to learn his laws, and thereby to start the process of becoming like him. If we do not so begin we shall never receive the promised reward.

Because God stands revealed or remains forever unknown, and because the things of God are known only by the power of the Spirit, perhaps we should redefine a mystery. In the gospel sense, a mystery is something beyond *carnal* comprehension.

The Saints are in a position to comprehend all mysteries, to understand all doctrine, and eventually to know all things. These high levels of intelligence are reached only through faith and obedience and righteousness. A person who relies on the intellect alone and who does not keep the commandments can never, worlds without end, comprehend the mystery of godliness.

There is probably more ignorance and confusion as to the mystery of godliness than there is about any other doctrine. As set forth in the three creeds of Christendom—the Nicene, the Apostles', and the Athanasian, which God himself said were an abomination in his sight—and as defined in the articles of religion of the various denominations, this doctrine is a mass of confusion and a mountain of falsity.

Even in the Church, thanks to a lack of knowledge and to intellectuality and the worldly enticement to conform to the general beliefs of an apostate Christendom, there are those who have fallen prey to many false delusions about deity. By way of illustration let us note some of the problems.

WHO AND WHAT IS GOD?

Is there a God? If so, who or what is he? Is he the laws and forces of nature? Or an image of mud or gold? Or is he Baal, the resurrected son of El to whom the Canaanites offered human sacrifices? Is he Allah or Buddha or the confusing and contradictory nothingness described in the creeds of Christendom?

Is there such a thing as the Trinity in which the Father, Son, and Holy Ghost are three gods and yet one god, a god who neither hears, nor speaks, nor appears, as did the one worshipped by the ancients?

Is God omnipotent, omniscient, and omnipresent, or are these descriptive designations part of the legends of sectarianism?

Are there three gods or one? Why does Jesus say his Father is greater than he and Paul say Jesus is equal with the Father? Why the great scriptural emphasis on proclaiming that three gods are one, and that the Lord our God is one Lord?

What of the mystery of our Lord's birth? Indeed, why should God even have a son? Is Jesus the Son of Man, or the Son of God, or is there a difference? Was it necessary to have a Savior and Redeemer, or is the Koran correct in teaching that God had no need for a son because Allah has but to speak and a thing is done?

By what power could Jesus atone for the sins of the world, or rise from death's dark tomb, or ascend physically into heaven? Is the atonement truly infinite and eternal, applying to all worlds and all created things?

Why does an angel say to John, "I am Alpha and Omega," and when John falls at his feet to worship him, say: "See thou do it not:

I am thy fellowservant, and of thy brethren that have the testimony of Jesus: worship God" (Revelations 1:8, 19:10)?

Why does Jesus say: I am the Son of God, and I said such and such unto mine Only Begotten, when in fact the Only Begotten is the offspring, not of the Son, but of the Father?

Why does Christ say: I am the Father and the Son and I created man in mine own image—when in fact Christ is the Son and not the Father, and when man was created, not by the Son, but by the Father?

What relationship do we have with the Lord? Do we worship the Father and him only, or do we also worship the Son? Should we seek for some special relationship with Christ, or does the plan of salvation call for us to seek the Spirit and thereby gain a oneness with both the Father and the Son?

All these are but sample questions, questions that raise some of the issues relative to the mystery of godliness.

UNDERSTANDING THROUGH THE POWER OF THE SPIRIT

It is our friend Paul who tells us: "Without controversy great is the mystery of godliness: God was manifest in the flesh, justified in the Spirit, seen of angels, preached unto the Gentiles, believed on in the world, received up into glory" (1 Timothy 3:16).

We agree. But all these things are beyond carnal comprehension. God dwelling in the flesh! How can anyone understand such a pronouncement unless quickened by the power of the Spirit?

The revealed word to Joseph Smith announces that endless torment does not last forever, and that eternal damnation is of limited duration. In spite of the plain meaning of words, the divine word is that eternal punishment and endless punishment do in fact have an end.

"For, behold, the mystery of godliness, how great is it," the Lord says, as he gives to these words a special scriptural definition. As he says, this is done so that the concepts involved "might work upon the hearts of the children of men, altogether for my name's glory" (D&C 19:6–12).

As it is with such a mystery as God dwelling in the flesh, or as eternal punishment having no reference to the duration, but rather to the kind of punishment, so it is with all else embraced within the designation *the mystery of godliness*.

The doctrine is what the doctrine is, and the concepts are what the concepts are. It is of no moment whatever that they spread confusion among uninspired worshippers at diverse shrines, or among intellectuals whose interest in religion is purely academic and who rely on the power of the mind rather than the power of the Spirit for understanding.

Gospel truths are known and understood only by the power of the Spirit. Eternal life—which is to know God—is such an infinitely great reward that men must study, ponder, and pray, with all their hearts, to gain the needed knowledge.

The Lord gives his truths line upon line and precept upon precept to those who believe and obey. Saving truths come by revelation to prophets, not by reason to false priests or doctors of debate, dissension, and divisiveness.

Let us, then, consider the mystery of godliness from the Lord's standpoint, setting forth correct principles, which will enable all who are spiritually enlightened to keep themselves on the proper path.

Let us do so with courage and without fear, but in reverence and with an open mind. If we are contrite and receptive, if we truly desire truth, and if we are guided by the Spirit in our search, we shall come off triumphant. We shall embrace every true principle and shunt every false doctrine back into the enveloping darkness from whence it came.

SEARCH DEEPER AND DEEPER

As we walk the razor's edge—the razor that divides truth from near truths, which sometimes have a pleasing attraction—let us be mindful of these words of the Prophet Joseph Smith: "The Savior has the words of eternal life. Nothing else can profit us. . . . I advise all to go on to perfection, and search deeper and deeper into the mysteries of Godliness" (*Teachings*, p. 364).

Let us ponder these basic concepts:

1. God is the Supreme Being. He is the only supreme and independent being in whom all fulness and perfection dwells. He is the Creator, Preserver, and Upholder of the universe and all that in it is. He is without beginning of days or end of life, and by him all things are. He is the object of all proper worship and from him all good gifts flow. He presides over and governs all things and therefore has no equal. That there is and can be only one supreme being is axiomatic. There can be three equal beings who possess the same character, perfections, and attributes, but there is and can be only one who is supreme, who is the head, and to whom all others are subject.

2. He is a holy man and has a body of flesh and bones. It is written: "No unclean thing can dwell . . . in his presence; for, in the language of Adam, Man of Holiness is his name, and the name of his Only Begotten is the Son of Man, even Jesus Christ" (Moses 6:57). That is, he is Ahman, and the name of his Only Begotten is Son Ahman.

And as it was with Jesus, the Son, who came forth in the resurrection with a glorified, immortal, resurrected body of flesh and bones, so it was with his Father before him. Joseph Smith said: "God himself was once as we are now, and is an exalted man, and sits enthroned in yonder heavens!" (*Teachings*, p. 345). Truly, truly, it is written: "The Father has a body of flesh and bones as tangible as man's" (D&C 130:22).

3. He is the Eternal Father, the Father of Spirits. God lives in the family unit and is the Father of spirits, of spirit men and spirit women, hosts of whom are now being born as mortal beings. He is, "Our Father which art in heaven" (Matthew 6:9). We are his children, and we are governed by his laws and are subject to his chastisement, all of which caused Paul to say: "We have had fathers of our flesh which corrected us, and we gave them reverence: shall we not much rather be in subjection unto the Father of spirits, and live?" (Hebrews 12:9).

4. He is omnipotent, omniscient, and omnipresent. Let there be no mistake about this. God has all power; he is the Almighty. He knows all things, and there is nothing in all eternity, in universe upon universe, that he does not know. Joseph Smith so taught, and all our scriptures, ancient and modern, bear a concordant testimony. He is not a student god, and he is not progressing in knowledge or learning new truths. If he knows how to create and govern worlds without number, and all that on them is, what is there left for him to learn? Also, he is omnipresent, meaning that by the power of his spirit he is in all things and through all things and round about all things.

5. What is the nature of God's life? The name of the kind of life that God lives is eternal life. One of his names, speaking in the noun sense, is Eternal, and he simply uses that name to describe the kind of life he lives. Eternal life consists of two things: (1) life in the family unit and (2) having the fulness of the Father, which is all power in heaven and on earth. It is because God has eternal life that he became the Father of Spirits as well as the creator and governor of all things.

6. Whence came the plan of salvation? It is simply the laws and ordinances by obedience to which men may gain eternal life and thus become as God is and be gods in their own right. Joseph Smith said: "God himself, finding he was in the midst of spirits and glory, because he was more intelligent, saw proper to institute laws whereby the rest could have a privilege to advance like himself. . . . He has power to institute laws to instruct the weaker intelligences, that they may be exalted with himself, so that they might have one glory upon another, and all that knowledge, power, glory, and intelligence, which is requisite in order to save them in the world of spirits" (*Teachings*, p. 354).

7. Who are Elohim and Jehovah? They are the Father and the Son. The Everlasting Elohim is the Great God by whom all things are; the Eternal Jehovah is his Firstborn in the spirit and his Only Begotten in the flesh. Jehovah is thus our Elder Brother, and as such was subject to the same plan of salvation, the plan given of Elohim for the salvation of all his children.

While yet in the premortal existence, Jehovah advanced and progressed until he became like unto God. Under the direction of the Father he became the Creator of worlds without number, and thus was himself the Lord Omnipotent.

8. Christ was chosen in the premortal existence as the Savior and Redeemer. After the Father had presented his plan of salvation to all his spirit children, after it had been taught so that all understood that what Elohim proposed would enable his spirit children to gain eternal life, after all the hosts of heaven had been taught what they must do in connection with their coming mortal probation—after all this the Father of us all called a Grand Council. We were all present to hear his voice and to accept or reject the proposal he then made.

In that council he said: "Whom shall I send to be my Son, to work out the infinite and eternal atonement, to put into full operation all of the terms and conditions of my plan to save my children." There were two volunteers—a conforming and obedient Jehovah and a rebellious and disobedient Lucifer.

The choice was made and the decree sent forth. The Father named his Beloved and Chosen One; he chose the Lord Jehovah who was the Creator of all things and who was then the Lord Omnipotent. He would be the one born as the Lord Jesus Christ. And this Chosen One was then foreordained and acclaimed as the Lamb slain from the foundation of the earth.

9. Man was created and commanded to serve the Father. It is written: "He created man, male and female, after his own image and in his own likeness, created he them; And gave unto them commandments that they should love and serve him, the only living and true God, and that he should be the only being whom they should worship" (D&C 20:18–19).

Please let these words of scripture sink into your heart and do not be confused about them. In order to gain salvation, we worship the Father and him only. He created us, he provided the plan of salvation, he called Christ to be the Savior and Redeemer, and he is the one that we and Christ shall be like if we are true and faithful in all things. We shall refer hereafter to the sense in which we worship Christ.

10. Man fell, became mortal, and entered a probationary estate. Created in a paradisiacal state in which there was no disease nor sorrow nor death—a state of innocence in which he could have no joy for he knew no misery, in which he could do no good, for he knew no sin—man, in conformity with the divine purpose, fell.

Temporal and spiritual death entered the world. Man became mortal. For the first time he could procreate and provide bodies for the spirits yet in the premortal existence. Truly, "Adam fell that men might be" (2 Nephi 2:22–25). We entered a probationary estate in which we are tried and tested to see if we will do all things whatsoever the Lord our God shall command us.

11. The Father provided a Savior and Redeemer. The eternal plan of salvation consists of the Creation, the Fall, and the Atonement. The Father having created man in his own image, and Adam having fallen that mortal man might enter his probationary estate, it but remained for the Father to provide a Savior and Redeemer. This he did in the person of his Only Begotten.

Thus Christ came into the world to ransom men from the temporal and spiritual death brought about by the fall of Adam. Thus all men are redeemed from the temporal death through the resurrection. All became immortal. "As in Adam all die, even so in Christ shall all be made alive" (1 Corinthians 15:22). And thus all men may be redeemed from spiritual death if they believe and obey, if they are true and faithful, if they keep the commandments.

12. Christ is the Mediator. Man in his fallen state is forever lost unless he rises from the Fall and regains the spiritual life that once was his. He must return to that God from whose presence he departed when he left the paradisiacal confines of Eden. Christ's mission is to bring to pass this reunion. He mediates the cause of the children of men so they can once again be in harmony with their Maker.

"God our Saviour," Paul tells us, "is willing to have all men to be saved." In order to be saved, he says, they must "come unto the knowledge of the truth which is in Christ Jesus, who is the Only

Begotten Son of God." He is the one who is "ordained to be a Mediator between God and man."

Then our ancient apostolic friend makes this great declaration: "For there is one God, and one mediator between God and men, the man Christ Jesus; Who gave himself a ransom for all" (JST, 1 Timothy 2:3–6).

Ponder this concept: There is one God, one Supreme Being, one above all who dwells in heaven. He appointed a man—Christ Jesus, Paul calls him—to be a mediator between the Father and his fallen children. And this mediator, though serving as a man when he atoned for the sins of the world, has now become as his Father and reigns with him in everlasting glory.

13. The gospel is the plan of reconciliation. Through the mediation of Jesus Christ it is within the power of fallen man to be reconciled with the Father. Christ's ministry is one of reconciliation; as he is a mediator, so he is a reconciler. And we as his servants are appointed to labor in a like manner.

Paul tells us that God "hath reconciled us to himself by Jesus Christ, and hath given to us the ministry of reconciliation." This doctrine is, he continues, "that God was in Christ, reconciling the world unto himself, not imputing their trespasses unto them," on conditions of faith and repentance. And he "hath committed unto us the word of reconciliation," making us, thus, "ambassadors for Christ" and enabling us to say to all men: "We pray you in Christ's stead, be ye reconciled to God" (2 Corinthians 5:18–20).

14. Christ is our advocate. We have an advocate, eternal in the heavens, one who knows our infirmities, our sufferings, and our sorrows because he too was subject to the flesh and suffered beyond our comprehension while he dwelt as a man. Indeed, he was "a man of sorrows, and acquainted with grief," and he bore "our griefs, and carried our sorrows" (Isaiah 53:3–4).

These are his words as he now pleads our cause in the courts above: "Father, behold the sufferings and death of him who did no sin, in whom thou wast well pleased; behold the blood of thy Son which was shed, the blood of him whom thou gavest that thyself might be glorified; Wherefore, Father, spare these my brethren that believe on my name, that they may come unto me and have everlasting life" (D&C 45:4–5).

15. Christ is the God of our Fathers. He is the God of Adam, and Enoch, and all of the Saints who were before the flood. He is the God of Abraham, Isaac, and Israel, and of all the holy prophets. As Jacob the Nephite said,

We knew of Christ, and we had a hope of his glory many hundred years before his coming; and not only we ourselves had a hope of his glory, but also all the holy prophets which were before us.

Behold, they believed in Christ and worshiped the Father in his name, and also we worship the Father in his name. [Jacob 4:4–5]

Thus all of the ancient Saints—all those from Adam to Noah, and from Noah to Abraham, and from Abraham to Moses, and from Moses to the coming of Jesus in the flesh—all of the truly faithful ones of old had the gospel. They were baptized and received the gift of the Holy Ghost; they were endowed with power from on high; they received the blessings of celestial marriage. The gospel is everlasting, and all men in all ages are saved by obedience to the same laws and the same ordinances.

16. Christ is the Promised Messiah. For 4,000 years—from Adam to John the son of Zacharias—all of the prophets foretold the coming of the Messiah, the Deliverer, the Holy One who would deliver his people, redeem the faithful, and ransom all men from death, hell, the devil, and endless torment. All of the ancient saints testified of a Christ who would come to bring to pass the immortality and eternal life of man, even as we testify of a Risen Lord who has taken captivity captive and opened the gates of heaven to all who believe and obey.

17. The mystery of the birth of our Lord. To those with spiritual insight and understanding, there is no mystery. The Lord Jehovah, the Firstborn spirit, Son of the Father, was born as the Lord Jesus. God was his Father and Mary was his mother. He was the Only Begotten in the flesh. From his Father, who is a holy man, he inherited the power of immortality, which is the power to live everlastingly; from his mother, a choice and chosen vessel of the lineage of David, he inherited the power of mortality, which is the power to die.

Thus, being dual in nature, he was able to lay down his life and to take it again. Thus he gave up the ghost at Golgotha, and three days later took up his partially embalmed and anointed body as it lay lifeless in an Arimathean's tomb.

18. Christ ministered among mortals. Though our Blessed Lord came into the world to die upon the cross for the sins of the world, though that was the chief intent and purpose of his mortal ministry, though his assigned ministry was to atone for the sins of the world—yet, while he was here, he restored the fulness of the gospel to the earth and taught its doctrines through all Judea and Galilee and beyond.

But, be it remembered, the gospel he taught originated with God his Father. "My doctrine is not mine," he said, "but his that sent me. If any man will do his will, he shall know of the doctrine, whether it be of God, or whether I speak of myself" (John 7:16–17).

19. Christ worked out his own salvation. This is something of which uninspired men have no comprehension. Truly, he was the Lord Omnipotent before the world was; truly, he was like unto the Father in the premortal life; truly, he was the Son of God here on earth—and yet, with it all, as with all the spirit children of the same Father, he too was subject to all of the terms and conditions of the Father's plan.

He also was born on earth to undergo a mortal probation, to die, to rise again in immortal glory, to be judged according to his works, and to receive his place of infinite glory in the eternal kingdom of his Everlasting Father. How well Paul said:

Though he were a Son, yet learned he obedience by the things which he suffered;

And being made perfect, he became the author [that is, the cause] *of eternal salvation unto all them that obey him.* [Hebrews 5: 8–9]

20. Christ worshipped the Father. This also is something that is seemingly unknown in the sectarian world. Of course our Blessed Lord, the Lord Jesus himself, the one who is our Savior and Redeemer, of course he worshipped the Father. How else could he (not having received the fulness at the first, as John tells us) go from grace to grace until he received the fulness of the glory of the Father?

Why else would he say to Mary Magdalene as she bowed before him on the resurrection morning: "Go to my brethren, and say unto them, I ascend unto my Father, and your Father; and to my God, and your God" (John 20:17)? Note it and note it well—Elohim is the God of Jehovah as truly and as fully as he is our God. And as Christ worshipped the Father, so must it be with us if we are to go where Christ is and be like him, according to the promises.

21. Christ—the Atoning One and the Crucified One. That which happened in Gethsemane and at Golgotha constitutes a mystery we cannot comprehend. We do not know how a God could bear the sins of all men on conditions of repentance. We cannot fathom the agony involved when Jesus, suffering both body and spirit, sweat great drops of blood from every pore. We only know that it was part of the plan of the Father and that our Lord drank to the full the cup that was his.

In Gethsemane, perhaps for three hours or more, and then again during the final three hours on the cross of Calvary, in agony beyond comprehension or compare, Jesus worked out the infinite and eternal atonement. For our purposes it suffices to know that this ordeal, plus his rising in glorious immortality, has brought to pass the immortality of all men and made eternal life available to all the obedient.

22. Christ—the Resurrected One and the Ascended One. As the sun crowns the day and banishes the darkness of the night, so the resurrection crowns the Atonement and forever abolishes the death that otherwise would have been eternal. Out of the agonies of the one came the glory of the other.

Christ our Lord rose in glorious immortality, the firstfruits of them that sleep, and then, ascending to his Father, he received all power in heaven and on earth. And in a way incomprehensible to us, the effects of his resurrection shall pass upon us all, and we too shall have power, if true and faithful in all things, to ascend to heights beyond the stars.

Now, if time and circumstances permitted, we might continue our presentation and add another score or a hundred headings to those so far named—all shedding light upon that which is mysterious to the carnal mind.

Perhaps you should continue the inquiry, resolving such mysteries as the following:

How the Holy Ghost can be a personage of spirit and yet convey his gifts to millions of mortals at one and the same time.

What eternal covenant was made relative to man—by God the First, and God the Second, and God the Third—before the foundations of the earth.

How and in what manner we worship Christ when the revealed word decrees that we should worship and pray to the Father and to him only and to none other.

How and in what manner the Lord Jesus both worships the Father and is an equal to him.

What is meant by the numerous scriptures that say Christ is the Father as well as the Son.

Why angels sometimes speak in the first person as though they were Christ, and why Christ himself often speaks in the first person as though he were the Father.

Why our great goal in life should be to gain the Spirit of the Lord as our companion, and what results will flow from such an attained eventuality.

And so on and so on and so on.

The scriptures are in our hands. The door to investigation and research and learning is never closed. We are all expected to learn the same truths, live the same laws, and open the same door to the same mysteries.

For thus saith the Lord—I, the Lord, am merciful and gracious unto those who fear me, and delight to honor those who serve me in righteousness and in truth unto the end.

Great shall be their reward and eternal shall be their glory.

And to them will I reveal all mysteries, yea, all the hidden mysteries of my kingdom from days of old, and for ages to come, will I make known unto them the good pleasure of my will concerning all things pertaining to my kingdom.

Yea, even the wonders of eternity shall they know, and things to come will I show them, even the things of many generations.

And their wisdom shall be great, and their understanding reach to heaven; and before them the wisdom of the wise shall perish, and the understanding of the prudent shall come to naught.

For by my Spirit will I enlighten them, and by my power will I make known unto them the secrets of my will—yea, even those things which eye has not seen, nor ear heard, nor yet entered into the heart of man. [D&C 76:5–10]

Now this work in which we are engaged is true. And the doctrines which we proclaim are God's eternal truth. And as the Lord lives, they will endure in time and in eternity. He has placed us here in a mortal circumstance and commanded us to seek him and to strive to be like him. He has given us an abundant amount of revealed truth in the holy scriptures. They are before us; they are available to each of us on the same basis. The prophet said that God has not revealed anything to Joseph that he will not reveal to the Twelve and to the least and last Saint as soon as he is able to bear it.

My prayer is that we, the rising and young generation in whose hands the future and destiny of the Church lies for the decades and ages that are ahead before the second coming of the Son of Man, will take the challenge and search deeply and learn the mysteries of godliness and let them be the standard around which we rally and be the guide that directs our lives in all that we do. If this be our course, we will surely have peace and joy and happiness in this life, and be inheritors of eternal life in the world to come, which may God grant for all of us, in the name of Jesus Christ. Amen.